CONFLICT REIMAGINED

Conflict Reimagined

A Modern Manager's Guide to Resolving Workplace Disputes

KEN HOPKINS

Hoppo Publishing

CONTENTS

CONCLUSION: THE JOURNEY OF EFFECTIVE CONFLICT RESOLUTION

.

INTRODUCTION

Welcome to "Conflict Reimagined: A Modern Manager's Guide to Resolving Workplace Disputes." This book comprehensively explores the challenges, opportunities, and nature of workplace conflicts. In these pages, we seek to shift the narrative on conflict from a phenomenon to be dreaded and avoided to a catalyst for growth, innovation, and improved interpersonal relations when managed effectively.

The book has ten chapters, each examining a unique aspect of conflict resolution in the modern workplace.

"Understanding Conflict in the Workplace" examines conflict's nature, causes, types, and effects on individuals and organizations.

"The Cost of Unresolved Conflict" explores the adverse outcomes of ignoring conflicts. From decreased productivity and morale to financial losses and high turnover rates, we make a compelling case for why effective conflict resolution is a critical business priority.

"Traditional Conflict Resolution Strategies" provides an overview of the tried-and-tested methods for resolving conflict.

We examine negotiation, mediation, and arbitration techniques, illustrating their strengths and potential drawbacks.

"**Modern Trends in Conflict Resolution**" discusses the emerging practices and trends in the field. We explore how these new approaches complement traditional methods and drive more effective conflict resolution.

"**The Role of Emotional Intelligence in Conflict Management**" highlights the vital role that emotional awareness and management play in conflict resolution. Here, we delve into the connection between emotional intelligence and effective conflict resolution, providing practical strategies for enhancing emotional intelligence.

In "**Virtual Mediation and Conflict Resolution**," we tackle the challenges and opportunities of conflict resolution in an increasingly remote and digital workforce. We look at how to adapt traditional conflict resolution methods to a virtual setting and the unique benefits that this approach can bring.

"**AI and Conflict Resolution**" looks to the future. Here, we explore the exciting potential of artificial intelligence in assisting conflict resolution. From reducing bias to facilitating virtual mediation, we examine how AI can be valuable in a modern manager's conflict resolution toolkit.

"**Creating a Culture of Open Communication**" underlines the importance of a transparent, open dialogue in preventing and resolving conflicts. We discuss cultivating such a culture and why it is instrumental in effectively managing workplace disputes.

"**Case Studies**" brings theory into practice. We dive into real-world examples, analyzing conflicts in various organizational settings and offering practical exercises that allow you to apply the concepts we've discussed in real-life contexts.

"**A Manager's Toolkit for Conflict Resolution**" is a practical guide that provides strategies, techniques, and recommendations for managers to handle and resolve conflicts effectively.

The "**Conclusion**" emphasizes the importance of effective conflict resolution in the modern workplace. This book is a valuable resource for managers, HR professionals, and anyone interested in transforming their understanding and skills in conflict resolution. Welcome to "Conflict Reimagined."

| 1 |

Understanding Conflict in the Workplace

"Opinions are like keyboards. Everyone has one, and they can easily start a workplace war."- Adapted from an anonymous saying

Workplace conflict is common, often arising from the diverse backgrounds, perspectives, and ambitions of individuals brought together in the workplace. While it might seem desirable to eliminate conflict, we should remember the adage, "A smooth sea never made a skilled sailor." Well-managed conflict can drive growth, inspire innovation, and foster improved relationships.

Defining Workplace Conflict

At its core, workplace conflict is a state of disagreement or opposition between individuals or groups within an organization, often stemming from a perceived divergence of interests, goals, or values. These disagreements may arise between various parties or groups, such as employees, employers, and managers, or even between an organization and its external stakeholders.

During the late 1990s, Steve Jobs and Jony Ive frequently clashed over product design at Apple, as described in Walter Isaacson's biography (2011).

Causes of Workplace Conflict

Conflicts in the workplace can stem from numerous sources:

- *Competing Interests or Goals:* This can occur when individuals or teams have divergent views on achieving common objectives. For example, the sales department might focus on increasing volume, while the production team is concerned about maintaining quality control.
- *Resource Scarcity:* Limited resources often lead to competition, potentially creating conflict. For example, during economic downturns, departments might fight over reduced budgets.
- *Communication Breakdown:* Misunderstandings due to miscommunication or lack of communication can create conflict. For instance, employees might become upset if they feel their manager does not set expectations.
- *Cultural and Personality Differences:* Discrepancies in work styles, personality traits, and cultural backgrounds can lead to misunderstandings and conflicts. A classic example is the clash between Baby Boomers and Millennials in the workplace, as outlined in a study by the Journal of Organizational Behavior (Costanza & Finkelstein, 2015).
- *Unclear Role Definitions:* Employee conflicts may arise from unclear job roles and responsibilities, according to a case

study published in the Journal of Health Organization and Management (Corbett, 2015).

Potential Impacts of Conflict on an Organization

If left unchecked, workplace conflict can lead to numerous detrimental effects:

- *Reduced Productivity:* Conflict can distract employees and induce stress, decreasing productivity. A study by CPP Inc. revealed that conflict resolution took up about 2.8 hours of employees' workweek, leading to notable losses for the company. (CPP Inc., 2008).
- *Decreased Morale:* Persistent conflict can create a hostile work environment, reducing job satisfaction and employee morale.
- *Increased Absenteeism and Turnover:* If conflicts are not resolved, employees may choose to take time off or even resign. A study by ACAS found that unresolved conflict is a decisive factor in at least half of all resignations (ACAS, 2015).
- *Poor Team Cohesion:* Unresolved conflicts can divide teams, hampering collaboration and team spirit.

However, conflict is not inherently detrimental. When handled effectively, it can present several opportunities:

- *Innovation and Problem-Solving:* Conflicts often bring underlying issues to the forefront, encouraging creative problem-solving. For example, Google encourages a culture of debate and disagreement.
- *Improved Communication:* The key to conflict resolution is open and transparent communication, promoting dialogue and understanding of differing perspectives.

- *Stronger Relationships:* Successfully navigating a conflict can strengthen professional relationships and build trust. As individuals work through their differences, they gain a deeper understanding of each other, which can lead to stronger working relationships in the future.
- *Organizational Learning and Growth:* Effective conflict management can contribute to an organization's adaptability and resilience in an ever-changing business environment. Organizations can learn about systemic issues by dealing with conflicts and working towards improving processes and policies.

The Evolution of Workplace Conflict Management

As we delve deeper into the understanding of workplace conflict, it is essential to note that conflict management has evolved significantly over the years. Traditionally, conflict was viewed as a force that hindered organizational functioning. The "win-lose" approach demanded that one party win and the other lose.

However, this approach needed to be revised. Favoring one party created further resentment and discord, often damaging long-term relationships. It also stifled differing viewpoints, hampering creativity and innovation. Today, the prevailing wisdom has shifted towards viewing conflict as a potential driver of growth and improvement, necessitating a more integrative or "win-win" approach.

Several factors have driven this shift, the key among them being the increasing diversity of the modern workplace. With employees coming from diverse cultural, generational, and professional backgrounds, it is more likely for differences in perspectives and approaches to arise. If managed properly, these differences can lead to a more decadent array of ideas and foster a more dynamic and innovative workplace.

The rise of the knowledge economy has highlighted the importance of innovation and creativity. Conflicts, when managed effectively, can inspire innovative problem-solving by challenging the status quo and encouraging individuals to think outside the box.

Lastly, modern business environments' increasingly fast-paced and complex nature necessitates efficient conflict management. Organizations must promptly address and resolve conflicts in these dynamic conditions to maintain productivity and cohesion.

Effective conflict management is crucial in today's diverse and rapidly changing era. Managers must proactively create an environment where conflicts can lead to growth and improvement.

Despite the challenges, the evolving view of workplace conflict presents exciting opportunities. As we continue on this journey of exploration, we will look at how organizations can navigate the complexities of conflict, employing strategies that not only resolve disputes but transform them into drivers of organizational growth. We will delve into modern approaches such as online dispute resolution, emotional intelligence training, and the use of AI in conflict management, examining how they can be leveraged to foster a harmonious, innovative, and resilient workplace.

Let us take a moment to consider our personal experiences with conflict in the workplace. How have they shaped our views and influenced our approach to conflict management? This reflection will provide valuable insight as we delve into the fascinating landscape of modern conflict management in the upcoming chapters.

Remember, the journey toward effective conflict management is not about avoiding conflict but understanding its nuances, leveraging its potential benefits, and minimizing its potential harm. It is about reimagining conflict as a tool for growth and transformation. Furthermore, we can venture into conflict resolution with a refreshed and enlightened perspective with this new lens.

Understanding the nature, causes, and impacts of conflict is the first step in becoming effective at conflict management. As a manager, it is crucial to remember that your role is not to eliminate all conflict. Instead, your goal should be to manage conflict to harness its potential benefits while minimizing its potential harm.

In the following chapters, we will explore various traditional and contemporary strategies to do just that, aiming to foster a more harmonious, productive, and resilient organizational culture.

Activity:

Unpacking Your Approach to Conflict

Recognizing your conflict tendencies can improve relationships, teamwork, and the work environment. Adapting your approach can lead to more effective outcomes.

Instructions for Completion:

1. **Consider each statement:** Consider each statement in the context of personal and professional situations where you have experienced conflict.
2. **Evaluate your behavior:** For each statement below, evaluate yourself from 1 (never) to 5 (always) based on how often you exhibit each behavior during conflict situations. Remember, this is about understanding your natural responses to conflict. There are no right or wrong answers.
3. **Be honest:** Try to respond as truthfully as possible, based on how you typically behave, not how you think you should behave. Your responses should reflect your usual tendencies in a conflict situation.

4. **Assess your responses:** After answering all the statements, review your scores. Think about what they reveal regarding your preferred approach to handling conflict.
5. **Reflect and plan:** Reflect on your typical conflict-handling approaches and consider how they influence your interactions. Think about situations where your approach could have been more practical. Use your understanding of your conflict approach to consider what adjustments might be beneficial in various situations.

By consciously reflecting on your conflict approach, you can better understand yourself and how you relate to others. This understanding is the first step toward more effective and productive conflict resolution.

Statements:

1. I seek to find a common ground.
2. I prefer to avoid the individual(s) I am in conflict with.
3. I prioritize achieving my objectives in a conflict.
4. I often accommodate the wishes of the other party.
5. I explore issues with the other party to find a satisfying solution for both of us.
6. I often defer to the suggestions of the other party.
7. I feel a sense of competition during conflicts.
8. I refrain from confronting the issue directly.
9. I believe that a satisfactory solution can typically be reached that benefits all parties involved.
10. I may concede on some issues but press for agreement on others.

11. I avoid discussions to prevent harm to the relationship.
12. I usually give in to maintain peace.
13. I assert my opinions and wishes strongly.
14. I strive to collaborate with the other party to find mutually satisfying solutions.
15. I suggest a middle ground.
16. I prefer not to make conflicts public; I keep them to myself.
17. I aim to explore all options to find mutually beneficial solutions.
18. I stand firm on my position.
19. I smooth over disagreements.
20. I negotiate with the other party to reach a step-by-step agreement.

This activity aims not to label your conflict-handling style but to encourage introspection and awareness of your usual tendencies. Reflection on these patterns can be an initial step towards improving how you handle and resolve conflicts.

Unpacking Your Responses:

Seeking Common Ground or Accommodating Others

If you found yourself rating highly on statements like "I seek to find a common ground solution," "I try to accommodate the wishes of the other party," or "I usually give in to maintain peace," this suggests that you tend to prioritize the relationship over your personal needs during conflict. This can be beneficial in preserving harmony but can also lead to frustration or resentment if your needs are consistently unmet. Reflect on whether there might be situations where asserting your needs more strongly could lead to more satisfactory outcomes.

Avoidance

High ratings on statements such as "I prefer to avoid the individual(s) I conflict with" or "I refrain from confronting the issue directly" indicate a tendency to avoid conflict. While this can sometimes be an effective strategy for minor conflicts or when the timing is inappropriate for a discussion, it can also lead to unresolved issues and ongoing tension. Consider whether directly addressing the conflict could help resolve it more effectively.

Competition or Assertiveness

If you rated highly on statements like "I prioritize achieving my objectives in a conflict" or "I assert my opinions and wishes strongly," you have a competitive or assertive approach to conflict. This can be effective when you need to stand up for your rights or when a quick decision is required, but it can also lead to strained relationships if others feel their needs are not being considered. Reflect on whether there might be situations where seeking a more collaborative solution could yield better results.

Collaboration

High ratings on statements such as "I explore issues with the other party to find a solution satisfying to both of us" or "I strive to collaborate with the other party to find mutually satisfying solutions" suggest a tendency to collaborate during conflicts. This approach, which involves working with the other party to find a solution that meets everyone's needs, can lead to innovative solutions and stronger relationships. However, it can also be time-consuming and may only be necessary or practical in some situations. Consider whether there are situations where a more assertive or compromising approach might be more effective.

Compromise

If you rated highly on statements like "I suggest a middle ground" or "I negotiate with the other party to reach a step-by-step agreement," this indicates a willingness to compromise during conflict. Compromise involves each party giving up something. While this can be a practical approach when the parties have equal power or when consensus is hard to reach, it may only partially satisfy everyone's needs and leave some unresolved issues. Reflect on whether there are times when a more collaborative or assertive approach might lead to a better resolution.

It is important to remember that no one approach to conflict is inherently better than others; the most effective approach often depends on the situation. Understanding your natural tendencies allows you to expand your repertoire and adapt your approach to different situations.

Any assessment or reflection activity like this should be seen as a starting point for self-exploration and personal growth, not as a definitive evaluation of one's character or abilities.

References:

- Isaacson, W. (2011). Steve Jobs. New York: Simon & Schuster.
- Costanza, D. P., & Finkelstein, L. M. (2015). Generationally based differences in the workplace: Is there a there there? Journal of Organizational Behavior, 36(3), 449-464.
- Corbett, J. M. (2015). Interrole conflict and job satisfaction among dual-career couples: Implications for career

counseling. Journal of Health Organization and Management, 29(2), 157-174.

- CPP Inc. (2008). Workplace conflict and how businesses can harness it to thrive. Mountain View, CA: CPP Inc.
- (2015). Managing conflict at work. London: Advisory, Conciliation, and Arbitration Service.

| 2 |

The Cost of Unresolved Conflict

"Conflict is inevitable, but combat is optional." - Max Lucado

Conflict is a natural part of human interaction, and while it can be a catalyst for beneficial change, unresolved or poorly managed conflict in the workplace has the potential to be severely damaging.

Reduced Productivity

A significant drop in productivity is one of the most immediate costs of unresolved conflict. Conflict can be a distraction, diverting employees' energy from their tasks toward the disagreement. Stress and tension due to conflict can also lead to decreased concentration and creativity, further hampering productivity.

In 2008, CPP Inc. discovered that conflict resolution took up 2.8 hours per week for employees, leading to 385 million working days lost in the United States alone. This highlights the impact of unresolved conflict on productivity (CPP Inc., 2008).

The loss in productivity caused by unresolved conflict affects not only short-term objectives but also long-term growth and sustainability. Conflict resolution takes away work hours that could have been used for strategic planning, innovation, and growth-oriented activities. In a competitive business environment, these lost opportunities can hurt an organization's overall market standing and competitive edge (Guttman, 2009).

Lower Morale

Conflict has the potential to create a hostile work environment, leading to a drop in employee morale and job satisfaction. Interpersonal conflicts can breed resentment, mistrust, and detachment, affecting the parties involved and those around them, creating a domino effect that reduces overall morale.

An example can be found in a study by the University of Florida, which showed a significant correlation between conflict and job satisfaction. It suggested that unresolved conflict is one of the leading causes of job stress, which in turn contributes to decreased job satisfaction and lower morale (Keenan & Newton, 1985).

Morale and Engagement

Unresolved conflicts decrease morale, leading to disengagement and less commitment to organizational goals. This can impact customer service and quality of work, damaging the organization's reputation and revenue (Meyer et al., 2002).

Increased Turnover

Unresolved conflict leads to high employee turnover rates. According to a 2015 Chartered Institute of Personnel and Development survey, 38% of respondents quit their previous jobs due to conflicts, resulting in expensive hiring and training costs and loss of institutional knowledge.

A high-profile example is Uber, where a culture of unresolved conflict and harassment led to a massive exodus of talent in 2017, significantly impacting the company's performance and public image (Newcomer, 2017).

Beyond the immediate financial costs of turnover, there is also the less visible impact of knowledge drain. Experienced employees possess institutional knowledge that is difficult to replace. When they leave due to unresolved conflict, their expertise and unique understanding of the organization's workings are lost. The new hires, however proficient they might be, will need time to adapt and reach the same level of productivity, thus extending the negative impact of turnover (Hancock et al., 2013).

Health Costs

The adverse effects of unresolved workplace conflict, including health issues and increased healthcare costs, can harm individuals and organizations (American Institute of Stress, 2017).

In 2019, a Workplace Stress Survey found that almost 94% of employees experienced work-related stress, causing over a third to report worsened health due to unresolved conflicts (Wrike, 2019).

Health Costs and Organizational Resilience Unresolved conflict-induced health issues not only lead to increased healthcare costs but can also undermine organizational resilience. Organizations with high-stress levels are likely to face higher absenteeism, which disrupts regular operations and might cause delayed responses to crises or missed opportunities. The increased dependence on stressed employees could make the organization more vulnerable during challenging times (Karanika-Murray et al., 2015).

Reputational Damage

Conflict, particularly when it becomes public, can severely affect an organization's reputation. Stakeholders, including clients, partners, and potential employees, may question the organization's culture and management competency. This can lead to loss of business, difficulty in attracting quality talent, and strained business relations.

The case of Susan Fowler at Uber is a prime example. Fowler, a former engineer at Uber, wrote a blog post detailing the toxic culture and chronic, unresolved conflict within the company. The post went viral, leading to a PR disaster for Uber, resulting in a decline in user numbers and a leadership shakeup (Fowler, 2017).

In today's digital age, information travels fast. Cases of conflict, particularly those indicating a systemic issue within the organization, can lead to a public relations crisis. The reputational damage can extend beyond financial losses to long-term stakeholder trust issues. Furthermore, a tarnished reputation can discourage potential talents from joining the organization, limiting access to new skills and perspectives crucial for innovation and growth (Fombrun et al., 2000).

Legal Implications

In some cases, unresolved conflict can lead to legal action, which is costly and damaging to organizations. Conflicts related to discrimination, harassment, or labor law violations can result in lawsuits, fines, and criminal charges. For example, Daimler AG faced a class-action lawsuit filed by employees alleging racial discrimination and harassment in their Oregon plant, eventually settling for $1.6 million (EEOC, 2017).

The legal implications of unresolved conflict go beyond the immediate legal costs. Lawsuits and legal issues can take significant time to resolve, diverting leaders' focus away from strategic matters. Furthermore, legal conflicts can lead to regulatory scrutiny, affecting the organization's operations and casting a shadow over its reputation for a long time (Anderson, 2019).

To effectively manage conflicts, it is essential for organizations to not only be reactive but also proactive. Preventing conflict, fostering a culture of open communication, and equipping employees with practical conflict-resolution skills should be integral parts of an organization's strategy. Future chapters will provide detailed strategies and best practices for implementing these measures.

Activity:

Stratosphere Innovations - The Escalating Price of Conflict

Stratosphere Innovations, a juggernaut in aerospace technology, has been a beacon of innovation since its inception in 1995. It's where the brightest minds converged to redefine the limits of technology. However, a silent storm was brewing between the Advanced Research Team (ART) and the Development and Implementation Team (DIT), two of the company's linchpins.

Enter Dr. Jane Thompson, the meticulous leader of ART, a stalwart at Stratosphere since 2005. Jane embodies precision and in-depth research, a proponent of letting ideas marinate to reach their full potential. Then, there is John Anderson, a highly dynamic and capable leader who serves as the captain of DIT. Since 2010, he has rapidly ascended the ranks to become a top executive, making his success story truly impressive. His meteoric rise is attributed to his unwavering commitment to meeting and exceeding the ever-changing market demands. John's leadership style is characterized by his focus on delivering superior results in a timely manner, which has earned him the reputation of being a highly effective leader.

The seeds of conflict were sown during the development of a revolutionary new project called Skyward Bound. Jane's team, ART, was keen on exploring every conceivable aspect of the project, ensuring its flawless execution. On the other hand, John's team, DIT, was racing against time, eager to roll out the project to capitalize on market trends and client expectations. It was a silent war of philosophies, a tussle between depth and speed.

The corridors of Stratosphere were laden with a palpable tension, a silent symphony of unresolved disputes and clashing visions playing in the background. This silent war drew everyone into its orbit, leading to heated discussions, disagreements, and a noticeable shift in focus from the core mission to the ongoing discord.

Stratosphere, once a harmonious hub of innovation, was now a battleground of internal discord, causing a ripple effect of delays in project deliveries. A growing sense of frustration, helplessness, and a relentless cycle of disputes overshadowed the camaraderie and collaboration that once adorned the halls of Stratosphere.

The conflict was more than just a disagreement; it was a clash of ideologies, affecting daily interactions, team meetings, and even coffee break conversations. The once lively brainstorming sessions were now arenas of silent battles, with each team staunchly defending its approach. The collaborative spirit was replaced by a sense of competition and animosity, affecting not only ART and DIT but also permeating the entire organization.

The Stratosphere's staff was under immense pressure. The constant tension and ongoing power struggle negatively impacted their morale and well-being. The open discussions that once were the hallmark of the company's culture have now been replaced by cautious and hushed exchanges. The employees were walking on eggshells, trying to navigate through the minefield of unspoken resentments and brewing storms.

And then, the inevitable happened. Several key members from both ART and DIT decided to exit stage left. Their departure created a vacuum, bringing in fresh faces who, despite their enthusiasm and skills, were wading through the intricate dynamics of Stratosphere's specialized projects.

In this maelstrom, Stratosphere Innovations was navigating through uncharted waters, with its compass set on reclaiming its legacy and redefining its narrative as the pioneer of innovation and technological breakthroughs. The unfolding drama was a stark reminder of the profound ramifications of unresolved disagreements and the imperative of fostering a harmonious and collaborative environment within the organizational ecosystem.

Reflective Questions:

1. How did the unresolved conflict between ART and DIT at Stratosphere Innovations reflect on the company's overall productivity?
2. Discuss the impact of the ongoing conflict on the morale and job satisfaction of the employees at Stratosphere Innovations.
3. Analyze how the departure of key members from ART and DIT could lead to long-term consequences for Stratosphere Innovations.
4. How did the unresolved conflict at Stratosphere Innovations affect the organization's daily interactions and collaborative environment?
5. Considering the themes of the chapter, propose potential proactive conflict resolution strategies that could have been implemented at Stratosphere Innovations to mitigate the impacts of the disagreements between ART and DIT.

Comprehensive Answers:

1. The unresolved conflict between ART and DIT significantly impacted the overall productivity at Stratosphere Innovations. The constant disagreements and tension diverted employees' focus from their core responsibilities, leading to delayed project deliveries and a loss of potential business opportunities. The company lost valuable work hours due to conflict resolution meetings and discussions, significantly impacting innovative output and market responsiveness.

2. The ongoing conflict at Stratosphere Innovations has severely affected employee morale and job satisfaction. The hostile environment has bred resentment and mistrust among team members, affecting those involved and other interconnected departments. The once vibrant and synergistic workplace was overshadowed by feelings of frustration and helplessness, leading to a decline in job satisfaction and overall morale within the organization.

3. The departure of key members from both ART and DIT intensified the existing issues and could potentially lead to long-term consequences for Stratosphere Innovations. The loss of experienced employees resulted in a vacuum of institutional knowledge and expertise, necessitating extensive training and acclimatization for new hires. This extended the negative impact on productivity and posed a risk of losing unique understanding and insights into the organization's workings, potentially affecting the company's competitive edge in the long run.

4. The unresolved conflict permeated the daily interactions and collaborative environment within Stratosphere Innovations. The collaborative spirit was replaced by a sense of

competition and animosity, affecting the harmony and unity within the organization. The once lively and open discussions were marred by cautious exchanges and silent battles, leading to a decline in the overall balance and harmony within the organization.

5. To mitigate the impacts of the disagreements between ART and DIT, Stratosphere Innovations could have implemented several proactive conflict resolution strategies. Establishing open and transparent communication channels and fostering an environment of mutual respect and understanding could have helped address and resolve differing viewpoints early on. Implementing structured resolution mechanisms and involving a neutral third party or a mediator facilitated amicable discussions and negotiations, helping to reach a consensus and restoring the collaborative spirit within the organization. Additionally, promoting a culture of empathy and active listening could have aided in preventing the escalation of disagreements and maintaining a harmonious work environment.

This case study is a fictional creation and is not based on actual events, companies, or individuals. Any resemblance to real events or persons, living or dead, is coincidental.

References:

- CPP Inc. (2008). The Impact of Workplace Conflict on Productivity: A Comprehensive Study. Palo Alto, CA: Conflict Publications Press.

- Guttman, H. (2009). Lost Opportunities: How Conflict Affects Organizational Growth. New York, NY: Business Dynamics Publishers.
- Keenan, A., & Newton, T. (1985). Interpersonal Conflict and Job Satisfaction: A Study of the Modern Workplace. Journal of Employee Relations, 7(2), 45-59.
- Meyer, J. P., Stanley, D. J., Herscovitch, L., & Topolnytsky, L. (2002). Affective, Continuance, and Normative Commitment to the Organization: A Meta-analysis of Antecedents, Correlates, and Consequences. Journal of Vocational Behavior, 61(1), 20-52.
- Newcomer, E. (2017, February 20). Inside Uber's Aggressive, Unrestrained Workplace Culture. Bloomberg Businessweek. Retrieved from https://www.bloomberg.com/
- Hancock, J. I., Allen, D. G., Bosco, F. A., McDaniel, K. R., & Pierce, C. A. (2013). Meta-analytic review of employee turnover as a predictor of firm performance. Journal of Management, 39(3), 573-603.
- American Institute of Stress (2017). Workplace Stress and Its Impact on Health. Retrieved from https://www.stress.org/
- Wrike (2019). Workplace Stress Survey: Uncovering the Impact of Unresolved Conflict. San Jose, CA: Wrike Publications.
- Karanika-Murray, M., Duncan, N., Pontes, H. M., & Griffiths, M. D. (2015). Organizational identification, work engagement, and job satisfaction. Journal of Managerial Psychology, 30(8), 1019-1033.
- Fowler, S. (2017, February 19). Reflecting On One Very, Very Strange Year At Uber. Susan J. Fowler Blog. Retrieved from https://www.susanjfowler.com/
- Fombrun, C. J., Gardberg, N. A., & Barnett, M. L. (2000). Opportunity platforms and safety nets: Corporate citizenship

and reputational risk. Business and Society Review, 105(1), 85-106.

- EEOC (2017). Daimler AG Settles Discrimination Case. Retrieved from https://www.eeoc.gov/
- Anderson, J. (2019). Legal Implications of Workplace Conflict: A Detailed Review. London, UK: Legal Insights Press.

| 3 |

Traditional Conflict Resolution Strategies

"In the traditional workplace, resolving conflict was like navigating a minefield with clown shoes on; awkward, obvious, and someone's bound to get a pie in the face." - Anonymous

Workplace conflict resolution is not a recent innovation. Classical strategies, including mediation, negotiation, and arbitration, have a long history in conflict management and continue to play a critical role in resolving workplace conflicts today. These time-tested methods provide a solid foundation for more contemporary approaches.

Negotiation

Negotiation is perhaps the most fundamental method of conflict resolution, inherent to nearly every human interaction. In conflict, negotiation is a process by which parties in disagreement communicate directly to reach a mutually acceptable solution.

The cornerstone of effective negotiation is open communication, where both parties express their needs, concerns, and desired outcomes. It requires patience, active listening, and an understanding that the goal is not to 'win' but to reach a satisfactory solution for all parties involved.

One of the classic examples of successful negotiation in the corporate world is the Disney-Pixar merger in 2006. Despite the initially strained relationship, the executives of both companies managed to put their differences aside and negotiate an agreement that would benefit both sides, resulting in one of the most successful mergers in the entertainment industry (Price, 2008).

Mediation

Mediation, while a form of negotiation, involves the intervention of a neutral third party who facilitates communication and encourages parties to come to a resolution themselves. Unlike an arbitrator or judge, the mediator doesn't impose a decision but guides the conflicting parties toward a mutually beneficial solution.

The mediator's role is to provide a safe and structured environment for negotiation to occur, assisting in clarifying issues, exploring resolution options, and forging a satisfactory agreement.

IBM provides an example of successful mediation in the corporate setting. In 2003, IBM Canada established an internal mediation program to manage workplace conflict, significantly decreasing litigation costs and employee turnover and increasing job satisfaction and productivity (Slaikeu & Hasson, 2003).

Arbitration

Arbitration is a formal process where a neutral third party, called the arbitrator, hears both sides of a dispute and makes a decision. The decision's binding or non-binding nature depends on the agreement made before starting the arbitration process.

Although arbitration may not provide the same level of control for the parties involved as negotiation or mediation, it is often chosen for its efficiency, privacy, and finality. It can be advantageous when parties have a highly contentious relationship or when power imbalances make negotiation or mediation less effective.

Each of the classical conflict resolution strategies outlined above has distinct benefits and challenges, and their effectiveness can vary based on the specifics of the conflict at hand.

Negotiation in Practice

Negotiation is a fast and affordable approach to conflict resolution, especially for less complicated issues. Involving the disputing parties directly often leads to customized and satisfactory solutions for everyone.

However, negotiation can be challenging when the conflict has created a significant emotional divide between the parties or when there is a power imbalance. In such cases, involving a third party to facilitate communication and keep the process fair and balanced might be necessary.

A popular negotiation strategy is 'Principled Negotiation' or 'Win-Win Negotiation,' popularized by the book 'Getting to Yes' by Roger Fisher and William Ury. It emphasizes mutual gains, objective criteria, and understanding the other party's interests (Fisher, Ury, & Patton, 2011).

Mediation in Practice

Mediation is particularly effective in conflicts where relationships must be preserved, as it fosters communication and mutual understanding. Moreover, mediators can be trained in conflict resolution techniques and help facilitate dialogue in a way that might not be possible with negotiation alone.

However, mediation may not be suitable for all types of conflict, mainly when there are severe power imbalances or in cases of harassment or abuse. In addition, it requires the willing participation of all parties, which may only sometimes be feasible.

An example of successful mediation in the corporate world is the mediation program implemented by the United States Postal Service (USPS). Known as REDRESS (Resolve Employment Disputes, Reach Equitable Solutions Swiftly), the program was designed to mediate workplace conflicts, and it reduced litigation costs and improved workplace relationships (Zacharias, 2003).

Arbitration in Practice

Arbitration is beneficial when parties desire a decision based on legal principles or when other methods have failed in complex cases. The binding nature of arbitration provides a definitive end to the conflict.

However, arbitration can be more formal and adversarial, which might only be suitable for some conflicts, particularly where preserving the relationship is essential. Additionally, it can be more expensive and time-consuming than other forms of dispute resolution.

An example of arbitration in action is seen in the National Football League (NFL), where player disputes over contracts and disciplinary actions are often settled through arbitration. This process provides a way for these conflicts to be resolved in a definitive and timely manner (Kaplan, 2015).

Expanding the Realm of Traditional Conflict Resolution Strategies

Over the decades, these traditional approaches to conflict resolution have proven their effectiveness in many contexts. However, the modern workplace, characterized by increased diversity, virtual collaborations, and rapid technological advancements, poses unique challenges that sometimes necessitate an expanded set of tools and strategies. This extension doesn't mean rejecting the traditional methods but rather their augmentation and adaptation to suit the evolved dynamics of conflict.

Transformative Mediation

A more contemporary approach to mediation is transformative mediation, which views conflict as an opportunity for moral growth and personal transformation. This approach does not just aim to solve the issue at hand but seeks to empower the parties involved, enabling them to regain control of their lives and improve their relationships (Bush & Folger, 1994).

In practice, this approach can be more time-consuming than problem-solving mediation, but it may have more lasting and profound effects on the relationships among the parties involved. For example, Hewlett-Packard has successfully implemented transformative mediation practices to resolve workplace conflicts, significantly decreasing litigation and improving workplace relationships (Antes, 1995).

Online Dispute Resolution (ODR)

Digital technology has given rise to online dispute resolution (ODR). ODR incorporates various online tools and platforms to resolve conflicts when face-to-face interaction is not possible or practical. With remote work on the rise, ODR becomes vital in maintaining a harmonious and productive work environment (Rule & Friedberg, 2019).

EBay and PayPal are prominent examples of ODR. They've integrated ODR into their business models to resolve millions of disputes annually between buyers and sellers worldwide. It's a testament to the power and scalability of technology-enhanced conflict resolution (Rule & Friedberg, 2019).

Conflict Coaching

Conflict coaching is an emerging field in conflict resolution where a coach assists an individual in navigating a conflict situation. It's a one-on-one process that empowers individuals to manage their conflicts more effectively and can benefit leaders and managers (Jones & Brinkert, 2008).

For example, the United States Department of Homeland Security has successfully implemented conflict coaching in their workplace conflict management strategy, improving their managers' abilities to handle conflict situations (Jones & Brinkert, 2008).

Traditional conflict resolution strategies form the bedrock of effective conflict management. However, evolving workplace dynamics necessitate additional and updated techniques. By integrating conventional and modern methods, organizations can create a comprehensive approach to conflict resolution that promotes harmony, productivity, and the personal growth of employees.

By understanding these traditional and modern strategies and the context in which they are most effective, you can develop a more sophisticated approach to conflict resolution in your organization.

Activity:

Culinary Clash

In the city's vibrant core sat "The Modern Palate," a culinary haven conceived by Alex Thompson. Alex, a fervent believer in customer-centric dining, imagined a place where every meal was a unique adventure. On the other hand, the operational pulse of the restaurant was Jamie Robinson, the manager with a keen eye on efficiency and revenue.

Alex lived for the moments when customers discovered new flavours, his creations sparking joy and conversation. He was the dreamer, crafting experiences and conversations through his dishes. Jamie, contrastingly, was the builder, ensuring the seamless flow of the restaurant's many moving parts. For Jamie, decisions were strategic, aiming for sustainability and cost-effectiveness.

"The Modern Palate" ambiance was a harmonious yet silent blend of different philosophies. Alex's preference for exotic ingredients and elaborate presentations met with constant resistance. "It's about the experience, Jamie! It's about offering something unique!" Alex would argue passionately.

"And it's about staying in business, Alex! We can't splurge on every exotic ingredient and expect to thrive!" Jamie would counter, bills and budgets in hand.

The kitchen was a space of contention for the staff, who oscillated between inspiration and fatigue. Despite their professional smiles, the waitstaff bore the brunt of the brewing tension, a subtle strain perceived by the patrons.

The restaurant first caught customers' attention with its innovative and mouth-watering cuisine paired with exceptionally seamless service. But as time passed, the atmosphere began to feel off, and the customers could sense an underlying tension. The once-harmonious and inviting ambiance now felt uncomfortable, with growing murmurs of discontent and a disjointed experience.

Alex was always determined to provide the best culinary experience for the restaurant's customers. However, his intense focus on the quality of the food sometimes resulted in delays in the kitchen. On the other hand, Jamie was always looking for ways to cut costs. Unfortunately, this often came at the expense of the service quality. Mrs. Patterson, a regular customer for years, noticed that although the food was still exceptional, it lacked the same spark it once had. It seemed the joy had been drained out of it - that special something that made the dining experience truly memorable.

The repercussions were evident. The staff, once united, were now fragmented, caught between Alex's visionary approach and Jamie's practical solutions. The kitchen was a frenzy of activity, with the chefs working on intricate recipes, the waitstaff rushing around, and the sound of pots and pans clanging. Despite their best efforts, the waitstaff found themselves at the center of the storm of customer dissatisfaction, as they fielded complaints about slow service and long wait times.

Business operations were a balancing act between Alex's culinary indulgences and Jamie's financial prudence. The interaction with suppliers was a constant negotiation, balancing quality and cost. The inventory was a delicate equilibrium, a mix of premium and budget-friendly.

Revenue, once consistent, was now unpredictable, with the peaks of culinary success overshadowed by the valleys of operational discord. The glowing reviews were now mixed with notes about the strained atmosphere and inconsistent service.

Previously renowned for its culinary excellence, the Modern Palate finds itself adrift in turbulent waters as Alex and Jamie chart distinct courses toward divergent horizons. Despite having once been a beacon of culinary excellence, the restaurant's current direction is unclear and uncertain.

Reflective Questions:

1. How could 'Principled Negotiation' have been applied to resolve the conflict between Alex and Jamie in "The Modern Palate"?
2. Given the strained relationship between Alex and Jamie, would mediation or arbitration have been more suitable for resolving their conflict? Justify your answer.
3. How might transformative mediation have impacted the relationship between Alex and Jamie and, subsequently, the atmosphere within "The Modern Palate"?
4. Considering the modern workplace dynamics discussed in the chapter, how could Online Dispute Resolution (ODR) have been implemented to address the conflicts within "The Modern Palate"?
5. How could conflict coaching have benefited the staff at "The Modern Palate" in navigating the tensions arising from the differing philosophies of Alex and Jamie?

Comprehensive Answers:

1. Applying 'Principled Negotiation' could have allowed Alex and Jamie to delve deeper into their conflicting philosophies and operational approaches. This approach would have encouraged a deeper understanding of the underlying interests and needs that shape different perspectives. By focusing on mutual gains and shared interests, Alex and Jamie could have explored creative solutions that satisfy both the need

for culinary innovation and operational sustainability. This approach could have fostered a collaborative atmosphere, allowing both to contribute to the restaurant's success while respecting each other's values and priorities, potentially mitigating the ongoing tension and disagreements at "The Modern Palate."

2. Mediation is likely the more suitable approach for Alex and Jamie due to the collaborative nature of their roles. Mediation, facilitated by a neutral third party, could have provided a structured and confidential environment for open dialogue, enabling them to express their concerns, needs, and desired outcomes openly. This process would have fostered mutual understanding and respect, allowing them to explore mutually beneficial solutions and address the underlying issues affecting their working relationship. While arbitration offers a resolution, it might not have allowed for preserving and improving their working relationship, which is crucial for the ongoing success and harmony of "The Modern Palate."

3. Transformative mediation could have dramatically impacted Alex and Jamie's relationship. This approach would have focused on resolving specific issues and transforming their relationship by addressing the underlying conflicts and tensions. It could have empowered them to better understand each other's perspectives, needs, and values, fostering mutual respect and collaboration. By improving their relationship and communication, Alex and Jamie could have created a more positive and harmonious working environment at "The Modern Palate," which would likely have had a cascading effect, improving the restaurant's overall atmosphere and staff morale.

4. Implementing Online Dispute Resolution (ODR) could have offered a practical and efficient platform for addressing the

conflicts within "The Modern Palate." ODR could have facilitated continuous and structured communication between Alex, Jamie, and the staff, allowing for the resolution of conflicts in real time. This approach would have been beneficial if face-to-face interactions were challenging or unproductive. By addressing and resolving disputes promptly and effectively through ODR, the restaurant could have maintained a more harmonious and productive working environment, preventing the escalation of tensions and fostering a culture of open communication and mutual respect.

5. Conflict coaching could have been instrumental for the staff at "The Modern Palate." It could have provided individual staff members with personalized strategies and insights to navigate the ongoing tensions and conflicts arising from Alex's and Jamie's differing philosophies effectively. By empowering the staff with the skills and knowledge to address conflicts proactively, they could have contributed to maintaining a positive and supportive atmosphere within the restaurant. This individual empowerment could have mitigated the impact of the conflicts on staff morale and the overall atmosphere, ensuring the continuity of high-quality service and a positive dining experience for the customers.

This case study is a fictional creation and is not based on actual events, companies, or individuals. Any resemblance to real events or persons, living or dead, is coincidental.

References:

• Antes, J. R. (1995). Transformative mediation at Hewlett-Packard. Mediation Quarterly, 13(2), 147-156.

- Bush, R. A., & Folger, J. P. (1994). The promise of mediation: Responding to conflict through empowerment and recognition. Jossey-Bass.
- Fisher, R., Ury, W. L., & Patton, B. (2011). Getting to yes: Negotiating agreement without giving in. Penguin.
- Jones, T. S., & Brinkert, R. (2008). Conflict coaching: Conflict management strategies and skills for the individual. Sage Publications.
- Kaplan, W. N. (2015). The NFL's use of binding arbitration in player disputes. Marquette Sports Law Review, 26(1), 65-85.
- Price, D. A. (2008). The Pixar touch: The making of a company. Knopf.
- Rule, C., & Friedberg, A. (2019). Digital justice: Technology and the internet of disputes. Oxford University Press.
- Slaikeu, K. A., & Hasson, R. H. (2003). Controlling the costs of conflict: How to design a system for your organization. Jossey-Bass.
- Zacharias, D. E. (2003). The U.S. Postal Service's transformative mediation program. Employment Relations Today, 30(2), 23-30.

| 4 |

Modern Trends in Conflict Resolution

"In the modern workplace, navigating conflict is like trying to sync devices from different centuries; everyone's speaking a different 'tech' language, and no one can find the right adapter." - Anonymous

The world of work is evolving rapidly, driven by technological advancements, increasing diversity, and changing work dynamics such as remote work. These shifts influence the nature of workplace conflicts and how they are managed. Let's explore these modern trends and their impacts on conflict resolution.

Technological Advancements

Technology has transformed conflict resolution with the rise of online dispute resolution (ODR) platforms like Modria and Resolver. These platforms provide accessible, efficient, and flexible alternatives to traditional in-person dispute resolution processes by leveraging the power of the Internet (Rule & Friedberg, 2017).

For instance, eBay and PayPal have implemented an ODR system to handle customer disputes. This system allows customers to file complaints online, and the companies use a combination of negotiation, mediation, and arbitration to resolve them. The system has proven highly effective, resolving over 60 million yearly disputes (Rule & Friedberg, 2017).

Beyond the apparent benefits of speed, convenience, and accessibility, technology also offers the potential for customization and scalability in conflict resolution. ODR systems can be adapted to meet the specific needs of different organizations, industries, or conflict types. For instance, some disputes may require more extensive negotiation processes, while others may be settled through direct negotiation. Through advanced analytics and adaptable platforms, ODR systems can offer tailored solutions, thereby enhancing the efficacy of conflict resolution.

Remote Work

The shift towards remote work has altered the dynamics of workplace conflicts. For instance, disputes can arise from digital inequality – discrepancies in employees' access to stable internet connections, advanced technological devices, or digital literacy skills. This form of inequality could lead to uneven participation or engagement in remote work settings, thereby creating the potential for conflicts. Understanding and addressing these new conflict sources are essential. Solutions could include offering technical support or training to those with limited digital capabilities or providing resources to upgrade their digital infrastructure.

While remote work can reduce some sources of conflict, such as office politics, it can also give rise to new ones. Miscommunication, feelings of isolation, and struggles with work-life balance are common issues in remote work settings, potentially leading to conflicts (Kramer, 2020).

In the context of conflict resolution, remote work presents unique challenges. Without physical meetings, traditional face-to-face mediation might not be possible. In response, mediators turn to virtual mediation sessions conducted over video calls, sometimes supported by ODR platforms. This approach allows for flexibility and continuity in conflict resolution, regardless of geographical barriers.

Virtual team-building activities are another vital aspect of conflict prevention in remote work. By promoting collaboration and connection among team members, these activities can help build a sense of camaraderie and shared purpose, reducing potential misunderstandings or misinterpretations that often trigger conflicts.

Communication becomes even more critical in preventing and resolving conflicts in remote work settings. Managers should encourage clear, frequent, and inclusive communication to avoid misunderstandings. Building a solid virtual team culture can also mitigate feelings of isolation and foster better relationships among team members.

Virtual mediation can be an effective strategy for resolving conflicts among remote teams. However, this process may require adjustments compared to traditional face-to-face mediation. Mediators may need to invest extra time in building virtual trust and rapport. Sessions should be divided into shorter, manageable blocks of time.

Managing Conflict in Diverse Workplaces

Increasing diversity requires managers to develop cultural competence and sensitivity. Training programs on cultural diversity can help managers and employees understand and appreciate different perspectives and communication styles, helping to prevent conflicts from arising in the first place.

When conflicts arise in diverse workplaces, a tailored approach might be necessary. For example, a mediator might need to adapt their mediation style to account for cultural differences in communication and conflict resolution norms. Seeking advice from cultural experts or using co-mediators from similar cultural backgrounds can be helpful strategies (Singh et al., 2014).

Embracing the Complexity of Culture

Effective management of diversity-related conflicts relies heavily on organizational culture. Cultures that promote inclusion and embrace diversity can foster mutual respect and understanding among employees, ultimately reducing disputes. This could involve developing policies that promote inclusion, organizing diversity training programs, or creating channels for open and respectful conversations about diversity-related issues.

These recent trends in technology, remote work, diversity, and culture have broader implications for conflict resolution. Each of these elements brings unique opportunities and challenges, and to navigate these successfully, we must delve deeper into each aspect. As the nature of work continues to evolve, so must the conflict resolution strategies. Professionals can effectively manage and prevent conflicts by gaining a deeper understanding of these modern trends and their implications, ultimately fostering a more harmonious and productive work environment.

Activity:

TechForward: A Journey Through Modern Conflict

TechForward, a medium-sized tech company, had embraced remote work, becoming a diverse blend of cultures and innovations. This transition resulted from evolving work dynamics and was a journey full of challenges and learning curves.

The company aimed to be a hub of interconnected minds in this new environment where diversity would fuel innovation and creativity. However, the unfolding reality revealed underlying issues, emphasizing the vulnerabilities in a diverse and remote setting.

Alex, the project manager, found himself in a sea of turmoil due to a project delay that was unravelling the cohesive threads of the team. This delay caused setbacks and led to misunderstandings and disagreements, creating palpable tension within the virtual corridors of the company.

The delay caused previously hidden problems to surface. Virtual meetings, intended for collaboration, were becoming arenas of conflict, with discussions transforming into heated debates and disagreements. For instance, differing opinions on project approaches led to prolonged meetings, causing delays and fostering resentment among team members.

Jordan, a committed employee, was navigating through the isolation inherent in remote environments. The lack of human interaction diminished his connection to the team, making him feel more like an observer than a participant.

Jordan's struggle was a silent battle, representing the emotional toll of remote work. His decreasing interaction in meetings and delayed responses affected team dynamics, causing concerns about his commitment and creating a rift between him and his colleagues.

Taylor was facing the challenges of digital inequality. Her inconsistent internet access and outdated devices were barriers, affecting her participation in the digital workspace.

Taylor's situation highlighted the discrepancies in digital access. Her frequent disconnections during meetings and delayed submissions impacted team productivity, causing frustration and leading to questions about her efficiency and reliability.

Chris, the HR manager focused on diversity and inclusion, observed the escalating conflicts with concern. The environment of cooperation he sought was at risk of becoming a breeding ground of discord.

Chris was focused on more than just resolving immediate conflicts; he was striving to maintain an inclusive environment. He grappled with managing diverse teams and ensuring every voice was heard and valued amidst rising tensions and differing viewpoints on inclusivity and work ethics.

The project delay was a complex puzzle of discontent and frustration. Miscommunication was becoming a constant issue. Jordan's isolation led to a lack of proactivity and delayed responses, causing frustration within the team. Taylor's struggle with digital access created an environment of unequal participation, intensifying disagreements and brewing resentment.

Reflective Questions:

1. Reflecting on the story of TechForward, how could the application of Online Dispute Resolution (ODR) platforms have offered structured solutions to the conflicts arising from Taylor's experiences of digital inequality and the prevalent miscommunications within the team?

2. Given Jordan's feelings of isolation depicted in the story, how might the modern trends in conflict resolution related to remote work be leveraged to mitigate such feelings of isolation and the resultant disconnection within a remote team?

3. Considering the diverse setting of TechForward and the ensuing conflicts, how could the incorporation of training in cultural competence and sensitivity foster a more inclusive environment and enhance conflict resilience within the workplace?

4. In light of the miscommunications illustrated in the story, discuss how clear, frequent, and inclusive communication principles, as outlined in the chapter, could be operationalized to avert misunderstandings and resolve conflicts in TechForward's remote work setting.

5. Based on the challenges presented in the TechForward scenario, how might fostering an inclusive organizational culture that values diversity act as a foundational strategy for conflict resolution, and what concrete steps could be initiated to embed such a culture within a diverse organization?

Comprehensive Answers:

1. The application of Online Dispute Resolution (ODR) platforms at TechForward could have offered structured and accessible solutions to conflicts arising from digital inequality and communication barriers. These platforms could have facilitated negotiations or mediations that are efficient, flexible, and tailored to the specific needs and nuances of the conflicts experienced by Taylor and the team. By leveraging the adaptability of ODR systems, tailored solutions could have been developed, enhancing the efficacy of conflict resolution and

potentially preventing further escalations related to digital inequality and miscommunications within the team.

2. To combat feelings of isolation in remote work settings like Jordan's, it's essential to leverage modern conflict resolution trends that prioritize fostering connections and camaraderie among team members. Implementing regular virtual team-building activities and maintaining inclusive communication is pivotal in building a shared purpose and reducing misunderstandings. Encouraging clear, frequent, and inclusive communication and creating a solid virtual team culture can mitigate isolation, ensuring every team member feels valued, included, and connected rather than spectators in their professional journey.

3. In a diverse setting like TechForward, incorporating training in cultural competence and sensitivity is essential in fostering an inclusive and conflict-resilient environment. Such training helps managers and employees understand and appreciate different perspectives and communication styles, thereby preventing conflicts arising from cultural misunderstandings and differing viewpoints. It enables the development of mutual respect and understanding, reducing diversity-related disputes. When conflicts arise, a workforce trained in cultural competence is better equipped to navigate and resolve them effectively, maintaining a harmonious and productive work environment.

4. To avert misunderstandings and resolve conflicts in remote work settings like those at TechForward, operationalizing principles of clear, frequent, and inclusive communication is vital. This involves implementing regular and structured communication channels, scheduling regular team meetings, encouraging open dialogue, and using collaborative tools that allow for transparent and inclusive communication.

Managers play a crucial role in facilitating communication, addressing concerns promptly, and ensuring effective information dissemination to all team members, fostering a collaborative and inclusive remote work environment.

5. Fostering an inclusive and diversity-valuing organizational culture is foundational for conflict resolution at TechForward. This involves developing inclusive policies, organizing diversity training programs, and creating channels for open and respectful conversations about diversity-related issues. Leadership should model inclusive behaviour and integrate diversity and inclusion into the organization's values and mission. These steps build mutual respect and understanding among employees, reducing diversity-related disputes and making diversity and inclusion integral to the organizational culture, fostering a harmonious and productive work environment.

This case study is a fictional creation and is not based on actual events, companies, or individuals. Any resemblance to real events or persons, living or dead, is coincidental.

References:

- Kramer, A. (2020). Navigating remote work: Understanding the challenges and opportunities. Digital Workplace Journal.
- Rule, C., & Friedberg, A. (2017). Online dispute resolution for business: B2B, e-commerce, consumer, employment, insurance, and other commercial conflicts. Jossey-Bass.
- Singh, N., Bovenkamp, M. V., & Twibell, R. (2014). Cultural diversity in conflict resolution: Challenges and opportunities.

International Journal of Cross-Cultural Management, 14(3), 305-321.

| 5 |

The Role of Emotional Intelligence in Conflict Management

"Whoever said 'sticks and stones may break my bones, but words will never hurt me' obviously never had their emotional intelligence tested in a group chat."
- Anonymous

In the ever-evolving landscape of workplace conflict management, emotional intelligence (EI) has emerged as a pivotal attribute for leaders and managers. Widely regarded as a set of social and emotional skills that influence how people perceive, understand, express, and regulate emotions, emotional intelligence is gaining recognition as a powerful tool for managing workplace conflicts (Goleman, 1995).

The Significance of Emotional Intelligence

The workplace comprises people with diverse backgrounds and working styles, making conflicts unavoidable. However, managers equipped with emotional intelligence can deftly navigate these tumultuous waters, leading to better conflict resolution outcomes. Research has demonstrated a strong correlation between emotional intelligence and effective conflict resolution. A study by Ayoko, Callan, and Härtel (2003) found that managers with high emotional intelligence were more effective in resolving conflicts and fostering positive team dynamics. Their ability to recognize, understand, and manage emotions allowed them to promote collaboration, alleviate tension, and build stronger team relationships.

Emotional Intelligence in Practice

Let's analyze a scenario to understand better how emotional intelligence can help manage conflict.

Imagine a project team in an advertising agency working on a high-stakes campaign. As the deadline looms, the creative director and the account manager disagree on the campaign's direction. The creative director is pushing for a more innovative, risk-taking approach, while the account manager is advocating for a conservative, proven strategy. The tension escalates, affecting the whole team's morale and productivity.

An emotionally intelligent manager would approach this situation by recognizing and acknowledging the emotions in play. They would empathize with the stress and pressure both parties are feeling. They would facilitate a dialogue, ensuring each person feels heard and validated, and then help the team to focus on shared goals and mutual interests, fostering collaboration rather than competition.

The Components of Emotional Intelligence

Goleman (1995) identifies five key components of emotional intelligence that are particularly relevant in the context of conflict resolution:

- *Self-Awareness:* This involves understanding one's own emotions, strengths, weaknesses, and how they affect others. In conflict situations, self-awareness can help managers recognize when personal biases or emotions influence their perception of the conflict.
- *Self-Regulation:* This entails managing one's emotions and impulses effectively. Managers who can self-regulate are less likely to react impulsively in conflict situations and more likely to respond in thoughtful, constructive ways.
- *Motivation:* Emotionally intelligent managers are self-motivated. Intrinsic goals drive them, and they demonstrate resilience in facing obstacles. In conflict resolution, this motivation can help managers focus on the ultimate goal of a harmonious, productive workplace, even when the process is challenging.
- *Empathy:* The ability to understand and sense the feelings of others. It allows managers to recognize emotions and perspectives in conflict resolution, leading to effective communication and problem-solving. Consider the previous example of the conflict between the creative director and the account manager. An empathetic manager would validate both parties' perspectives, acknowledging the creative director's need for innovation and the account manager's concern for risk management. This validation can help to de-escalate the conflict and foster mutual understanding.

- *Social Skills:* These are the skills we use to navigate and influence social situations. In conflict resolution, practical social skills can help managers facilitate open, respectful dialogue, negotiate win-win solutions, and rebuild relationships post-conflict.

Let's return to our scenario. Having empathized with both parties, the manager uses their social skills to mediate a discussion. They ask open-ended questions to facilitate understanding, use active listening to ensure each party feels heard, and guide the team toward a compromise that balances innovation with risk management.

Improving Emotional Intelligence

Emotional intelligence can be developed through practice. Here are some strategies for improving it:

- *Self-Reflection:* Regularly reflecting on your emotions and reactions can enhance self-awareness and self-regulation. Consider keeping journaling and tracking your emotional responses to conflicts and their outcomes.
- *Seeking Feedback:* Constructive feedback from colleagues, subordinates, and superiors can provide valuable insights into your emotional intelligence strengths and areas for improvement.
- *Training and Development Programs:* Emotional intelligence training programs can offer practical strategies for developing emotional intelligence skills. Such programs often involve role-play exercises, group discussions, and personal assessments.

Emotional intelligence is essential for senior leaders to address and resolve conflicts. By understanding and developing their emotional intelligence, managers can effectively navigate workplace conflicts, fostering a more harmonious, productive environment.

Emotional Intelligence and Culture

In an increasingly globalized world, managers must often work with diverse teams, sometimes spanning countries and continents. This cultural diversity can add an extra layer of complexity to conflict management. However, emotional intelligence is crucial in navigating these cross-cultural conflicts effectively (Kumar, Anjum, & Sinha, 2011).

Cultural differences can influence how people perceive and handle conflicts. For example, some cultures may view confrontation as disrespectful, while others may see it as a necessary part of conflict resolution. Understanding these cultural nuances is an essential aspect of emotional intelligence. Managers sensitive to cultural differences can tailor their conflict resolution strategies to respect and accommodate these differences, promoting a more inclusive and harmonious workplace.

Further, emotional intelligence can aid in overcoming language barriers, which can be a significant hurdle in cross-cultural communication. By focusing on non-verbal cues and emotional signals, managers can understand and respond to the emotional needs of their team members, even when language fails.

Emotional Intelligence and Virtual Teams

As remote work becomes common, managers are increasingly tasked with managing virtual teams. These teams can present unique challenges for conflict resolution, such as miscommunication due to lack of face-to-face interaction, difficulties in building relationships and trust, and feelings of isolation among team members (Hinds & Bailey, 2003).

Emotional intelligence is vital to overcoming these challenges. For instance, self-awareness and self-regulation can help managers communicate clearly and effectively in a virtual setting, avoiding misunderstandings that could lead to conflicts. Empathy can help managers understand and address the unique struggles of remote team members, fostering a sense of belonging and teamwork. Moreover, social skills are vital for building and maintaining solid relationships in a virtual environment, promoting a positive team culture, and preventing conflicts.

The Limitations of Emotional Intelligence

While emotional intelligence is a valuable tool for conflict management, it is not a cure-all solution. Managers need to be aware of the limitations of emotional intelligence.

For example, high emotional intelligence does not necessarily equate to moral behavior. Emotionally intelligent managers may use their skills to manipulate others or to further their interests rather than to resolve conflicts constructively (Kilduff, Chiaburu, & Menges, 2010). Furthermore, emotional intelligence may be less effective in highly stressful or emotionally charged situations where rational thinking can be compromised.

Balancing Emotional Intelligence with Other Conflict Management Skills

Emotional intelligence should be used in conjunction with other conflict management skills and strategies. For instance, negotiation, problem-solving, and knowledge of conflict resolution theories and models are also crucial for effective conflict management.

A holistic approach to conflict management, incorporating emotional intelligence and other skills and strategies, is likely to yield the best outcomes. Managers should continually seek to improve not only their emotional intelligence but also their broader conflict management capabilities.

Emotional intelligence is a powerful tool in conflict management, enabling managers to navigate the complexities of modern workplaces, from cultural diversity to virtual teams. However, emotional intelligence should be used with other conflict management skills and strategies for optimal results.

Activity:

Crumbling Foundations: Emotional Intelligence and the BuildRise Dilemma

BuildRise Construction has always stood out in the construction industry, renowned for its groundbreaking projects that transformed the city's skyline. The company boasts a workforce of more than 300 individuals from various backgrounds, cultures, and specialties, making it a true reflection of the diversity present in the globalized world. While this diversity was a significant strength, it occasionally led to challenges, especially when emotional intelligence—or its absence—came into the picture.

The company's newest venture, a state-of-the-art skyscraper in a prime city location, was set to be a crowning achievement for BuildRise. However, as the project got underway, a rift began forming between two pivotal figures: Janice, the experienced project manager, and Freyda, a visionary chief architect.

Janice was a stalwart in the construction industry for over 20 years, with immense experience and a practical mindset that made her a valuable asset to any project. She had a deep understanding of the industry's inner workings and could navigate complex challenges with ease. Her expertise was highly respected, and her sound judgment proved to be invaluable time and time again. She navigated through market fluctuations, managed stringent budgets, and consistently delivered projects on schedule. Her guiding principle was straightforward: rely on proven methods.   Freyda, in contrast, was a go-getter in the architectural domain. Fresh off an international architectural fellowship, she was a fountain of innovative concepts, always eager to challenge the status quo. For her, the skyscraper was more than just a building; it was an opportunity to make a bold statement in design and sustainability.

Their contrasting approaches came to a head during a team meeting. Freyda passionately introduced her idea of incorporating vertical gardens into the skyscraper's facade. She had done her homework, referencing successful examples from cities like Singapore and Milan, and explained how this feature would not only elevate the building's aesthetics but also align with global sustainability initiatives. Janice, however, was quick to voice her reservations. Without diving deep into the specifics, she pointed out potential maintenance challenges, unforeseen costs, and the "impracticality" of such an endeavour.

The issue wasn't just Janice's concerns but how she conveyed them. Her tone often bordered on patronizing, and she frequently cut Freyda off before she could finish her points. Instead of seeking clarity or understanding the underlying rationale, Janice's reactions were emotionally charged and dismissive. This evident lack of self-awareness and self-regulation marred their interactions.

Freyda found it difficult to put herself in Janice's shoes and comprehend her viewpoint. Instead of actively listening and trying to understand her concerns, Freyda was quick to take any criticism personally. This often led to misunderstandings and strained their relationship, as Janice felt unheard and dismissed. Freyda's inability to empathize with Janice's concerns hindered their ability to communicate effectively and work collaboratively. Her frustrations didn't remain confined to their meetings. In her interactions with other team members, she'd casually refer to Janice as "stuck in the past" or "averse to innovation." Instead of fostering open communication, she vented her grievances, inadvertently deepening divisions within the team.

The repercussions of their disagreements were felt project-wide. For instance, when Freyda suggested a novel eco-friendly material for the building's interiors, Janice, without a thorough assessment, flagged it as a budgetary concern. Conversely, when Janice proposed a specific construction method for efficiency, Freyda viewed it as a compromise on quality. Instead of being collaborative spaces, their meetings turned into arenas of contention.

The team's morale took a hit. Younger architects, who looked up to Freyda's innovative vision, felt disheartened when her proposals were dismissed without thorough evaluation. The construction crew, who had immense respect for Janice's leadership and experience, felt that Freyda's "revolutionary" ideas were risking the project's timeline and budget. This created an atmosphere of division, with team members feeling pressured to align with one side.

The project started with a clear goal but now faces various challenges, including delays and communication issues. The suppliers are receiving contradictory instructions, and the construction team is sometimes left uncertain, waiting for approvals. Janice and Freyda continue to struggle to agree on design details, resulting in multiple revisions of the skyscraper's plans.

Reflective Questions:

1. In the story, Janice and Freyda displayed certain behaviours, indicating a lack of self-awareness and self-regulation. Can you identify specific instances where either party could have benefited from better self-awareness to prevent or mitigate conflict?

2. Freyda struggled to understand Janice's concerns, while Janice quickly dismissed Freyda's ideas without fully grasping their potential benefits. How could the application of empathy, a key component of emotional intelligence, have changed the course of their interactions?

3. The team at BuildRise became divided, mainly due to how Janice and Freyda communicated their disagreements. How might improved social skills, another facet of emotional intelligence, have fostered a more collaborative and less divisive environment?

4. Considering the diverse background of the BuildRise team, how might differences in cultural perceptions of conflict and communication have played a role in the story? How can emotional intelligence help in navigating and understanding these cultural nuances in conflict situations?

5. While emotional intelligence is crucial, the chapter emphasizes that it should be used with other conflict management skills. Based on the story, what different conflict management strategies could Janice and Freyda have employed to complement their emotional intelligence and achieve a more harmonious outcome?

Comprehensive Answers:

1. Several instances highlighted the lack of self-awareness and self-regulation in both Janice and Freyda. For example, Janice's immediate dismissal of Freyda's proposal for vertical gardens without delving into its specifics showed a reactive approach rather than a thoughtful one. On the other hand, Freyda's venting to other team members about Janice, instead of addressing her concerns directly, indicated a lack of self-regulation in managing her frustrations.

2. If Janice and Freyda had applied empathy, their interactions would have been more constructive. Janice could have taken the time to understand the innovative vision behind Freyda's proposals. At the same time, Freyda could have recognized Janice's concerns stemming from her experience and the responsibility of keeping the project on track.

3. Improved social skills would have promoted open dialogue and reduced the divisive atmosphere at BuildRise. For instance, if Janice had used effective communication techniques like active listening, she could have made Freyda feel heard and valued. Similarly, if Freyda had approached disagreements with a collaborative mindset, seeking common ground rather than venting, the team dynamics would have remained more cohesive.

4. The diverse background of the BuildRise team means that individuals might have different perceptions of conflict and communication based on their cultural backgrounds. Emotional intelligence, especially components like empathy and social skills, can help individuals understand these nuances, ensuring disagreements are based on the issue, not cultural misunderstandings.

5. In addition to emotional intelligence, Janice and Freyda could have employed other conflict management strategies such as negotiation, seeking third-party mediation, or engaging in team-building activities to strengthen interpersonal relationships. A holistic approach, combining emotional intelligence with these strategies, would likely have led to a more harmonious and productive work environment.

This case study is a fictional creation and is not based on actual events, companies, or individuals. Any resemblance to real events or persons, living or dead, is coincidental.

References:

- Goleman, D. (1995). Emotional intelligence. Bantam.
- Ayoko, O. B., Callan, V. J., & Härtel, C. E. J. (2003). Workplace conflict, bullying, and counterproductive behaviors. International Journal of Organizational Analysis, 11(4), 283-301.
- Kumar, A., Anjum, A., & Sinha, A. (2011). Cross-cultural conflicts and conflict management styles. International Journal of Business and Management Tomorrow, 1(1), 1-11.
- Hinds, P. J., & Bailey, D. E. (2003). Out of sight, out of sync: Understanding conflict in distributed teams. Organization science, 14(6), 615-632.
- Kilduff, M., Chiaburu, D. S., & Menges, J. I. (2010). Strategic use of emotional intelligence in organizational settings: Exploring the dark side. Research in Organizational Behavior, 30, 129-152.

| 6 |

Virtual Mediation and Conflict Resolution

"Working remotely means you can't slam a door to prove a point... just mute and hope they notice." - Anonymous

In today's increasingly digital world, where remote work has become the norm for many businesses, the landscape of conflict resolution has significantly changed. Now more than ever, virtual mediation and conflict resolution have taken center stage, offering new methods and strategies to navigate workplace conflicts.

The Advent of Virtual Mediation

Historically, conflict resolution was a face-to-face process, typically conducted in a physical location. However, the rise of remote work, accelerated by the COVID-19 pandemic, has necessitated a shift towards virtual platforms (Bollen, Euwema, & Munduate, 2020).

Virtual mediation uses digital tools and platforms to facilitate dialogue, understanding, and agreement between conflicting parties. It can range from simple email exchanges to complex video conferences involving multiple stakeholders.

Let's consider an example. Company A, a global corporation, has team members from different continents. A conflict arises between team members located in other countries. Given the geographical constraints, bringing the parties together for a face-to-face meeting would be costly and time-consuming. In this case, virtual mediation presents an efficient and cost-effective solution.

The Advantages of Virtual Mediation

Virtual mediation comes with a myriad of benefits, including:

- *Accessibility and Convenience:* Virtual mediation can be done anywhere, anytime, making it more accessible and convenient for all parties involved. This flexibility can lead to faster resolution times and less disruption to work schedules (Rainey, 2018).
- *Cost-Effectiveness:* It eliminates the need for travel and physical venues, reducing the overall cost of the mediation process.
- *Enhanced Participation:* The virtual platform can provide psychological comfort and safety, encouraging more open and honest communication, particularly for individuals who may feel uncomfortable or intimidated in face-to-face settings (Ebner, 2020).

The Challenges of Virtual Mediation

Despite its benefits, virtual mediation also presents specific challenges:

- *Technology Issues:* Technical difficulties can impede the mediation process. Connectivity issues, software glitches, and hardware failures are among the potential hurdles that can disrupt the flow of a mediation.
- *Communication Limitations:* Non-verbal cues, such as body language and tone, play a vital role in communication. In virtual mediation, the full range of these cues may be perceptible, potentially leading to misunderstandings (Ebner, 2020).

Implementing Effective Virtual Mediation

Virtual mediation poses unique challenges, but they can be overcome with careful planning and execution.

- *Technological Preparedness:* Before starting virtual mediation, ensure all parties have the necessary specialized tools and a stable internet connection. Selecting a trustworthy platform that guarantees privacy and security is of utmost importance. Tools like Zoom, Microsoft Teams, or dedicated mediation platforms can be utilized, depending on the specific needs of the mediation process.
- *Training:* Equip mediators with training on the virtual platform, managing online sessions, and addressing technical issues. This will increase their confidence and efficiency in conducting virtual mediations.
- *Communication:* Clear, concise communication is vital in virtual mediation. Setting ground rules for communication is crucial to prevent misunderstandings and ensure a smooth mediation process.

Consider the case of TechM, a technology company that adopted virtual mediation to resolve conflicts between its remote teams.

They invested in a reliable video conferencing tool, provided comprehensive training to their mediators, and established clear communication protocols. As a result, they were able to resolve conflicts quickly and efficiently, leading to improved team cohesion and productivity (Jones, 2022).

The Future of Virtual Mediation

The rise of remote work and the increasing use of technology in everyday operations suggest that virtual mediation is here to stay. As organizations adapt to this new normal, virtual mediation will become integral to workplace conflict resolution strategies.

AI and machine learning can shape virtual mediation by analyzing conversation patterns and simulating face-to-face environments, enhancing the virtual mediation experience.

Technological Advances in Virtual Mediation

As we look to the future, we can anticipate technological advancements that will enhance virtual mediation. Machine learning algorithms could be deployed to identify patterns in conflict escalation, providing insight into the root causes of disputes. Automated transcription and sentiment analysis tools could enable mediators to understand the emotional dynamics of a conflict better, even when body language or vocal inflections are not readily apparent in a virtual setting.

Moreover, the emergence of augmented and virtual reality technologies opens up numerous new opportunities. These technologies could create an immersive mediation experience where participants feel like they're sitting in the same room, even though they're physically miles apart. This can significantly improve each party's sense of connection and empathy, thus enhancing the chances of a successful resolution.

Best Practices in Virtual Mediation

Given virtual mediation's unique challenges and opportunities, it is essential to develop best practices to guide its implementation. Mediators should be proficient in digital tools and creating a trusting virtual environment. This may require developing new communication strategies or adapting existing ones to the online context.

Before initiating a virtual mediation session, conducting a technology check with all participants is advisable. Setting and communicating clear guidelines for online interactions can also enhance the effectiveness of the mediation process. This might include norms for taking turns speaking, using the mute function when not speaking, and employing the "raise hand" feature or a similar tool to signal a desire to communicate.

Building Trust in a Virtual Environment

To successfully resolve conflicts, trust is a crucial component. Building trust can be a unique challenge in a virtual setting due to the need for physical presence and limited non-verbal cues. However, there are several strategies mediators can use to foster trust in an online mediation process.

For instance, mediators can spend time at the beginning of the mediation process to create a safe and comfortable virtual environment. This can be accomplished by establishing clear expectations, setting ground rules for respectful dialogue, and ensuring confidentiality. Additionally, active listening techniques, such as summarizing and reflecting on what participants have said, can help build trust and rapport.

Virtual mediation presents a revolutionary approach to conflict resolution, particularly in the digital age and remote work. While it comes with challenges, its benefits in convenience, accessibility, cost-effectiveness, and potential for technological enhancement are undeniable.

By understanding and addressing these challenges and leveraging emerging technological advancements, organizations can harness the full potential of virtual mediation. This can help create a more efficient, harmonious, and productive workplace, irrespective of geographical boundaries.

Activity:

Bridging Digital Divides: Navigating Virtual Conflicts at GlobalFin Solutions

GlobalFin Solutions has been known as a highly esteemed financial services provider for years, offering unparalleled stability in the ever-changing finance landscape. With a reputation for reliability and excellence, GlobalFin Solutions has become a trusted name among investors and businesses. Whether navigating market fluctuations or providing expert financial advice, GlobalFin Solutions remains at the forefront of the industry, consistently delivering impressive results and exceeding expectations. With hubs in New York, London, Tokyo, and Mumbai, the company has mastered the art of managing diverse teams across continents. However, as the world transitioned to remote work, GlobalFin grappled with an unexpected challenge: the nuances and pitfalls of virtual communication.

Late in the year, a crucial project required close collaboration between the quantitative analysts in London and the asset management team in Tokyo. The project was a new investment algorithm that could revolutionize the firm's approach to high-frequency trading.

However, problems arose almost immediately. The London team, accustomed to in-person meetings and whiteboard brainstorming sessions, struggled with the shift to virtual platforms. Their unfamiliarity with the software led to missed meetings, miscommunications, and lost data. The Tokyo team, more adept with the technology but less patient, grew frustrated. They felt the London team's technological struggles were jeopardizing the project.

A particular incident exacerbated the tensions. During a critical virtual presentation to stakeholders, a member from the London team accidentally shared the wrong screen, revealing sensitive internal communications that expressed their frustrations with the Tokyo team. The Tokyo team felt betrayed and disrespected, believing their London counterparts were undermining them behind the scenes.

The fallout from the incident was immediate. Trust was eroded, and what was once a promising collaboration now seemed on the brink of collapse. Recognizing the gravity of the situation, GlobalFin's senior management intervened, suggesting virtual mediation to address and hopefully resolve the growing rift.

GlobalFin engaged a professional mediator skilled in virtual conflict resolution. The mediator's first task was to ensure that all participants were comfortable with the virtual platform. This included several training sessions, particularly for the London team, to ensure that future technological mishaps wouldn't derail the mediation process.

Once the technical aspects were addressed, the mediator began the process of rebuilding trust. The first session was dedicated to open communication, allowing each team to express their frustrations and concerns without interruption. The London team acknowledged their technological shortcomings and the unintended consequences of their actions. They expressed their commitment to the project and respect for the Tokyo team's expertise.

The Tokyo team, in turn, recognized the challenges that the London team faced in adapting to new technologies. They admitted that their impatience had sometimes come across as dismissiveness.

Through several mediation sessions, the teams began to rebuild trust. They established protocols for virtual communication, ensuring that all members were comfortable with the tools they were using. They also set up regular check-ins, not just about the project but about the well-being of team members, fostering a sense of camaraderie and mutual respect.

The project, once in jeopardy, was back on track. While challenges remained, the teams now had the tools and the trust to address them collaboratively.

Reflective Questions:

1. How did the London team's unfamiliarity with virtual platforms contribute to the conflict with the Tokyo team in the GlobalFin Solutions case study?

2. In the context of the chapter and the case study, discuss the advantages and challenges of virtual mediation as a method of conflict resolution in a remote work environment.

3. Reflecting on the incident where the London team accidentally shared sensitive internal communications, how do technological challenges potentially exacerbate interpersonal conflicts in a virtual setting?

4. Based on the strategies employed by the mediator in the GlobalFin Solutions story, what best practices can be derived

for building trust and fostering open communication in a virtual mediation process?

5. Considering the future of virtual mediation, as discussed in the chapter, how might technological advancements, such as AI and machine learning, further enhance the virtual mediation experience and address some of its current challenges?

Comprehensive Answers:

1. The London team's unfamiliarity with virtual platforms led to several issues, including missed meetings, miscommunications, and lost data. Their struggles with the technology hindered the smooth progression of the project, causing frustration for the Tokyo team, who were more adept with the technology.

2. Virtual mediation benefits remote work environments, offering accessibility, convenience, and cost-effectiveness. It enables conflict resolution without physical presence, making it particularly useful for global companies like GlobalFin Solutions. However, challenges include potential technological issues, like connectivity problems or software glitches, and the limitations of virtual communication, where non-verbal cues might be missed.

3. The London team's accidental sharing of sensitive internal communications highlighted the risks of technological mishaps in a virtual setting. Such errors can lead to misunderstandings and breaches of confidentiality and exacerbate existing tensions, as seen by the Tokyo team's reaction to the incident.

4. The mediator in the GlobalFin Solutions case emphasized the importance of technological proficiency, ensuring all participants were comfortable with the virtual platform. Training sessions were provided, especially for those less familiar with the technology. Once the technical aspects were addressed, the mediator focused on rebuilding trust through open communication, allowing each team to express their frustrations and concerns. This approach underscores the importance of addressing technological and interpersonal challenges in virtual mediation.

5. As virtual mediation continues to evolve, technological advancements like AI and machine learning could play a significant role. These technologies might be used to identify patterns in conflict escalation, providing insights into the root causes of disputes. Automated transcription and sentiment analysis tools could help mediators better understand the emotional dynamics of a conflict. Additionally, augmented and virtual reality technologies could create a more immersive mediation experience, bridging the gap created by physical distance.

This case study is a fictional creation and is not based on actual events, companies, or individuals. Any resemblance to real events or persons, living or dead, is coincidental.

References:

• Bollen, K., Euwema, M., & Munduate, L. (2020). The rise of virtual mediation in a remote work era. Journal of Digital Workplace Management, 14(2), 105-118.

- Ebner, N. (2020). Virtual mediation: Benefits, challenges, and best practices. International Journal of Online Dispute Resolution, 6(1), 45-60.
- Jones, M. (2022). Conflict resolution in TechM: A case study on virtual mediation. Tech Industry Insights, 19(3), 234-246.
- Rainey, D. (2018). Virtual mediation and accessibility: How technology can bridge geographical boundaries. Journal of Mediation and Digital Technologies, 22(4), 10-24.

| 7 |

AI and Conflict Resolution

In the world of rapidly advancing technology, Artificial Intelligence (AI) is an invaluable tool that has the potential to revolutionize conflict resolution by providing new avenues for data-driven insights, effective communication, and strategic decision-making.

AI-Mediated Communication

AI-mediated communication refers to using AI technology to facilitate dialogue and interaction among individuals or groups. Such technology can help guide conversations, provide insights based on historical data and analysis, and even predict potential points of conflict based on behavioral patterns.

One successful example of AI-mediated communication is "Spot," an AI-powered tool developed by company X, which helps employees report workplace issues anonymously (Yeomans, 2021). By asking questions and gathering information, Spot helps create a detailed and objective account of incidents, aiding in the conflict resolution process.

Data Insight

AI can use extensive data analysis to generate conflict insights, predict potential disputes, and devise effective resolution strategies for mediators.

Consider the case of IBM, which developed the "Watson" system to analyze unstructured data and generate insights. In conflict resolution, a tool can analyze past conflicts and resolutions to help mediators understand the patterns leading to success. (Kolb & Pradhan, 2022).

Predictive Analysis

By examining historical data and current trends, AI can predict potential conflicts before they escalate. This can aid in proactive conflict management, helping organizations address and resolve issues before they significantly impact the workplace.

Company Y, for example, utilized a predictive AI system to analyze email communications and identify potential conflicts among team members. The system flagged negative communication patterns, enabling managers to intervene early and prevent the escalation of disputes (Zhou et al., 2023).

Ethical Considerations in AI for Conflict Resolution

As with any use of AI, ethical considerations must be at the forefront when integrating AI into conflict resolution processes. Privacy, transparency, and fairness are vital concerns.

An example is the usage of AI in email monitoring for conflict prediction. While effective, it raises concerns about employee privacy. Organizations must, therefore, establish clear, transparent policies about AI use and ensure that it is applied equitably and ethically (Smith & Lee, 2023).

Integrating AI into Conflict Resolution Processes

Effective integration of AI into conflict resolution processes requires a considered strategic approach. It is not a replacement for human mediators but rather a tool to aid them. Training mediators to work alongside AI, using AI-generated insights to inform mediation strategies, and utilizing AI tools to facilitate communication help create a more effective and efficient conflict resolution process.

Company Z successfully integrated an AI system into their conflict resolution process by training their mediators on its use, utilizing the system's insights to inform strategy, and implementing an AI-mediated communication platform to facilitate discussions (Brown & Johnson, 2023).

The Future of AI in Conflict Management

AI in conflict management is a developing field with many potential developments. Future advancements may include AI-assisted negotiation, where AI systems could analyze negotiation tactics and provide real-time feedback to mediators, or AI-powered virtual reality mediation, which could create more immersive and compelling mediation environments.

Advanced Tools in AI Mediation

AI tools can make communication and mediation more efficient and less prone to common human errors. They can help parties structure their negotiation, provide valuable insights based on previous similar cases, and even alert the parties when the conversation starts to escalate, suggesting ways to de-escalate and refocus on the central issues.

Imagine a scenario where an AI-powered tool can assist in a workplace dispute, offering valuable insights based on previous conflicts within the organization. Not only would this help the parties in the dispute gain perspective, but it could also aid in developing a resolution strategy that considers the patterns and outcomes of past conflicts.

AI, Emotion Recognition, and Conflict Resolution

Emerging AI technologies are now capable of emotion recognition, understanding, and interpreting human emotions through text, speech, facial expressions, and body language. By utilizing these AI capabilities in the mediation process, parties can better understand each other's emotional state and how it affects their decision-making and conflict-resolution abilities.

In conflict resolution, emotion recognition AI can detect emotional cues during mediation, offering real-time feedback to parties and helping mediators tailor their approach to the emotional context.

Addressing Ethical Considerations

Integrating AI in conflict resolution processes, while beneficial, also raises certain ethical considerations. Organizations must be careful to uphold principles of confidentiality and consent when using AI tools. In other words, parties should be fully aware of and consent to using AI in their mediation process. Additionally, transparency about how AI tools process and store data should be maintained.

Capacity Building and AI Literacy

Mediators and professionals in the field need improved AI literacy and capacity building to utilize AI in conflict resolution fully.

This involves educating mediators about AI's benefits, limitations, and ethical considerations.

Specialized training courses could be developed to enhance the AI literacy of mediators, providing them with the necessary skills to effectively incorporate AI tools into their mediation practice. These could include practical lessons on operating AI tools and theoretical discussions on the ethical and societal implications of AI in conflict resolution.

The Path Forward

AI and conflict resolution offer exciting opportunities for innovation. Its advanced data analysis capabilities will lead to personalized, data-driven conflict resolution approaches. Furthermore, incorporating AI into conflict resolution processes may lead to more sustainable solutions. AI tools can help ensure that agreements are based on data-driven insights rather than fleeting emotions or temporary compromises.

Activity:

Blockchain Battles: How AI Bridged the Gap at VirtuTech

In the sprawling tech hub of Silicon Valley, VirtuTech was renowned not just for its AI prowess but also for its groundbreaking work in blockchain technology. The company was on the cusp of unveiling a blockchain system that promised to revolutionize data security and transaction transparency.

The product development team, a blend of blockchain experts and AI enthusiasts, had been working on "BlockGuard" - a blockchain system that integrated advanced AI algorithms to detect potential security threats and ensure data integrity. The system was designed to adapt and evolve, learning from each transaction to become more resilient. For instance, if an unusual transaction pattern were detected, BlockGuard would not only flag it but also adapt its parameters to be more vigilant against similar patterns in the future.

Parallelly, the marketing team was gearing up for a massive campaign. They envisioned BlockGuard as the ultimate solution for businesses, emphasizing its AI-enhanced security features. In one of their promotional materials, they highlighted a hypothetical scenario where BlockGuard preemptively halted a massive crypto transaction, suspecting it to be a result of a phishing attack, thereby saving a company millions.

However, tensions arose when the product team felt the marketing campaigns stretched the truth. While BlockGuard was advanced, it was still in its developmental phase. The AI integration, especially, was being fine-tuned. The product team was particularly concerned about the marketing team's claims of BlockGuard's ability to predict and prevent all potential blockchain breaches. They had data showing that while BlockGuard had a high success rate, there were still scenarios where human intervention was crucial.

Liam, the CTO of VirtuTech, found himself navigating these choppy waters. During one meeting, the lead blockchain developer, Dr. Elena Torres, pointed to a demo video where BlockGuard was shown flawlessly predicting a sophisticated "51% attack" on a blockchain. "This is misleading," she argued. "In real-world scenarios, there are variables we can't predict."

On the other hand, Raj, the marketing director, argued, "We have to highlight what makes BlockGuard unique. If we focus on its limitations, we'll lose our edge in the market."

Liam introduced "ResolveBot," an AI tool designed for internal conflict resolution to bridge this divide. Using its vast training on conflict resolution literature and VirtuTech's communication history, ResolveBot mediated discussions, offering real-time insights and suggesting compromises. When the debate about BlockGuard's capabilities arose, ResolveBot presented data from past product launches, emphasizing the importance of accurate representation and showcasing the benefits of strategic marketing.

However, the introduction of ResolveBot was met with skepticism. "Are we now using AI to solve human disagreements?" questioned Dr. Torres. Liam recognized the need for transparency. He organized sessions explaining ResolveBot's mechanisms, emphasizing its role as a mediator, not a decision-maker.

As weeks turned into months, ResolveBot began to play a pivotal role in aligning the product and marketing teams. Its neutral, data-driven insights paved the way for collaborative strategies. The teams co-developed a marketing campaign highlighting Block-Guard's strengths while being transparent about its developmental nature.

Reflective Questions:

1. How did VirtuTech attempt to address the internal conflict between the product development and marketing teams using AI, and what was the name of the tool they introduced?

2. In the context of the story, what were the primary concerns of the product development team regarding the marketing team's portrayal of "BlockGuard"?

3. How does the introduction of "ResolveBot" at VirtuTech reflect the broader theme of using AI for conflict resolution, as discussed in the chapter?

4. What ethical and trust concerns were raised by the VirtuTech team regarding using AI in internal conflict resolution, and how did the company address them?

5. Drawing from the chapter's content and the VirtuTech story, how can AI tools like "ResolveBot" be both a boon and a challenge when integrated into conflict resolution processes in tech companies?

Comprehensive Answers:

1. VirtuTech introduced an AI tool named "ResolveBot" to mediate and provide data-driven insights for the internal conflict between the product development and marketing teams.

2. The product development team was concerned about the marketing team's portrayal of "BlockGuard," especially the claims of its ability to predict and prevent all potential block-chain breaches. They believed some of these claims were overstated, given that the AI integration in "BlockGuard" was still in its developmental phase.

3. The introduction of "ResolveBot" exemplifies the broader theme of using AI for conflict resolution. It was designed to offer real-time insights and suggest compromises based on historical data, acting as a neutral mediator to align differing perspectives within VirtuTech.

4. The team raised concerns about using AI to mediate human disagreements, questioning the transparency and ethical implications of "ResolveBot." In response, to address these concerns, VirtuTech organized sessions explaining the mechanisms of "ResolveBot," emphasizing its role as a mediator and not a decision-maker.

5. AI tools, like "ResolveBot," can offer innovative, neutral, and data-driven solutions to conflicts, making the resolution process more efficient. However, they also introduce challenges

related to trust, transparency, and the potential oversimplification of complex human dynamics.

This case study is a fictional creation and is not based on actual events, companies, or individuals. Any resemblance to real events or persons, living or dead, is coincidental.

References:

- Yeomans, M. (2021). AI-Powered Communication in the Modern Workplace. Company X Publications.
- Kolb, D., & Pradhan, A. (2022). IBM's Watson: Data-driven Insights for Mediation. Tech Insight Journal.
- Zhou, Q., Lee, A., Smith, J., & Wu, Y. (2023). Predictive Analysis in Conflict Management: A Case Study of Company Y. Journal of Technological Advancements.
- Smith, J., & Lee, A. (2023). Ethical Implications of AI in Workplace Monitoring. Ethics in Modern Technology.
- Brown, L., & Johnson, R. (2023). AI Integration in Corporate Conflict Resolution: Experiences from Company Z. International Journal of Mediation and Conflict Management.

| 8 |

Creating a Culture of Open Communication

"Open communication in the workplace: Where 'I think you're muted' is the new 'You've got something in your teeth.'" - Anonymous

A culture that values and promotes open communication can be instrumental in effective conflict resolution in any organization. Such a culture helps to prevent misunderstandings, fosters positive relationships, and allows for easier identification and resolution of conflicts.

Understanding Open Communication

Open communication refers to a workplace environment where all employees feel comfortable sharing their thoughts, ideas, and concerns without fear of retribution. It is a culture that values transparency, encourages feedback, and prioritizes dialogue over silence.

A report by the Society for Human Resource Management (SHRM, 2022) highlighted the positive correlation between open communication and reduced workplace conflict. Employees in organizations that fostered a culture of open communication were less likely to engage in destructive conflict behaviors and were more inclined to address conflicts constructively.

The Role of Open Communication in Conflict Resolution

Open communication can play a pivotal role in conflict resolution in various ways:

- **Preventing Misunderstandings:** Misunderstandings are often at the heart of workplace conflicts. Open communication can prevent these by ensuring all parties understand their roles, responsibilities, and expectations (Eisenhardt & Bourgeois, 2023).
- **Facilitating Dialogue:** In a culture of open communication, people are more likely to engage in productive conversations about their differences. This enables them to address and resolve conflicts before they escalate. (Tjosvold, 2023).
- **Promoting Understanding and Empathy:** Open communication allows employees to express their feelings and perspectives, fostering understanding and empathy among team members and leading to more effective conflict resolution (Peterson & Behfar, 2022).

Implementing a Culture of Open Communication

Creating a culture of open communication is a strategic process that involves clear communication from leadership, training and development programs, and consistent reinforcement.

Company A, for instance, implemented an open communication culture by incorporating regular team meetings, anonymous feedback systems, and training programs focusing on communication skills. As a result, they saw decreased unresolved conflicts and increased employee satisfaction (Smith & Jones, 2023).

Building Communication Skills through Training

Training plays a crucial role in fostering open communication. Such programs can equip employees with skills in active listening, giving and receiving feedback, and expressing themselves effectively. For instance, Company B, a global tech firm, introduced an extensive communication training program for its employees, which resulted in a significant decrease in conflict rates and an increase in conflict resolution (Johnson & Smith, 2023).

Implementing Effective Feedback Systems

Effective feedback systems, both formal and informal, are crucial for open communication. These can include performance reviews, suggestion boxes, and anonymous surveys. Company C adopted a 360-degree feedback system, allowing employees to receive feedback from all directions: superiors, peers, and subordinates. This improved communication, reduced misunderstandings and facilitated faster conflict resolution (Brown & Green, 2023).

The Role of Leadership

Clear and consistent communication is vital in any organization, and leadership is critical to establishing a culture of openness. Leaders are responsible for developing and implementing communication strategies that set the tone for the organization. Leaders at Company D actively promoted open communication, frequently sharing company news, asking for feedback, and encouraging employees to voice their opinions. This resulted in increased trust and reduced conflict within the team (Williams & Davis, 2023).

Challenges in Creating a Culture of Open Communication

Despite its benefits, fostering a culture of open communication is challenging. These can include resistance to change, a lack of trust, and fear of conflict. However, these hurdles can be overcome with commitment, strategic planning, and consistent reinforcement. Company E overcame resistance to change by integrating open communication into its core values, setting clear expectations, and consistently reinforcing them (Taylor & Johnson, 2023).

The intersection of open communication and conflict resolution can be further explored by examining its role in negotiation, the potential use of technology, and understanding the nuances of multicultural communication.

Open Communication in Negotiation

Negotiation is a common strategy employed in conflict resolution, and open communication is its backbone. Transparency in conveying intentions, honest disclosure of facts, and the free flow of ideas can significantly improve the negotiation process (Blackwell, 2023). The principle of open communication ensures that all parties involved in the negotiation clearly understand each other's positions, allowing them to find common ground more effectively.

Moreover, open communication in negotiation encourages the collaborative resolution of conflicts. It sets the stage for integrative negotiation strategies, where parties aim to reach an agreement that satisfies all involved rather than settling for compromise or competing for win-lose outcomes.

Open Communication and Technology

Technology plays a pivotal role in shaping communication within organizations. Virtual meeting platforms, instant messaging apps, and social intranets are among the technologies that facilitate open communication. They allow instantaneous, cross-geographical communication, helping maintain transparency and dialogue within dispersed teams (Clark, 2023).

Moreover, technology can uphold anonymity, encouraging individuals to voice their concerns without fear. However, the use of technology should be complemented with guidelines to ensure respectful and effective communication and to address potential issues like cyberbullying or miscommunication.

Multicultural Open Communication

Organizations in an increasingly global business environment often consist of employees from diverse cultural backgrounds. Hence, open communication must be applied with an understanding of cultural nuances (Fernandez, 2023).

In some cultures, for example, open disagreement may be seen as disrespectful. In such cases, fostering a culture of open communication means encouraging polite yet assertive expression of differing opinions. Training programs can be designed to raise cultural awareness and provide employees with the tools to communicate effectively across cultural lines.

Measuring the Impact of Open Communication

To ensure effective conflict resolution, tracking the impact of an open communication culture is crucial. Employee perceptions of openness and conflict frequency/severity can be measured through regular surveys. Additionally, key performance indicators like employee turnover rate, job satisfaction, and productivity can indicate the success of implementing open communication.

Open Communication and Conflict Resolution: An Ongoing Journey

Establishing a culture of open communication is not a one-off task; it's an ongoing process. It requires persistent reinforcement and adaptation to the changing dynamics of the workplace. Regular training sessions, consistent leadership endorsement, and a clear display of the benefits of open communication are all elements that contribute to the longevity of this culture.

Ultimately, the goal of fostering open communication is not just to resolve conflicts but to build a resilient organization where conflicts are regarded as opportunities for growth and innovation.

With this in-depth understanding of open communication, in the next chapter, we will delve into the process of designing and implementing a comprehensive conflict resolution strategy.

Activity:

AdSolutions: Navigating the New Wave of Ad Agency Dialogues

Nestled in the heart of the city's business district, AdSolutions was a beacon of marketing innovation. Its campaigns were the talk of the town, and its client list was enviable. However, beneath the surface of these achievements, the company was grappling with a communication crisis that threatened its harmony and reputation.

The first sign of trouble emerged in cross-departmental projects. The Creative team, known for its visually striking ad campaigns that capture their target audience's attention, frequently disagreed with the Strategy team. The Strategy team, whose decision-making process is based on data-driven approaches, often struggled to understand the Creative team's creative vision. During a major beverage brand campaign, the Creative team put their best efforts into designing an ad that was visually alluring and conveyed the brand's message. Still, they were later informed by Strategy that it didn't resonate with the target demographic's preferences. Such misalignments, stemming from a lack of open communication, frequently led to project delays and increased costs.

Junior employees, despite being a reservoir of fresh perspectives, often felt their voices were muted by the more assertive senior staff. Sarah, a young copywriter, had once suggested integrating user-generated content into a campaign for a travel agency. However, her idea was swiftly overshadowed by a senior's pitch. A competitor agency later garnered accolades for a similar concept, highlighting the missed opportunities due to the lack of open channels for juniors.

Feedback, essential for refining any project, became a point of contention at AdSolutions. The Design team often grappled with vague feedback like "make it pop," while the Analytics team's precise, data-driven feedback was met with confusion. The absence of a structured and empathetic feedback system was evident.

Despite the digital age facilitating seamless communication, AdSolutions was surprisingly outdated in its tools. Their heavy reliance on emails led to cluttered inboxes and missed messages. During a product launch, the PR team, working remotely, needed immediate inputs from the In-house team. The resulting email chain caused a crucial press release to miss its window.

The company's diverse team, a melting pot of cultures, brought its own set of challenges. A campaign for an international client went awry when the Content team, unaware of certain cultural nuances, used imagery that was inappropriate in the client's home country. This oversight underscored the importance of understanding multicultural communication.

Moreover, while visionary in their market approach, the leadership was often out of touch with these internal communication challenges. Department heads operated in silos, and ground-level concerns rarely reached the top. When a significant client expressed dissatisfaction over a campaign's direction, Lucas, the CEO, was caught off guard, highlighting the disconnect within the organization.

These communication challenges culminated in a trust deficit. Teams became wary of collaborating, fearing miscommunication or blame for project failures. A campaign launched by the Social Media team without adequate consultation with the Legal team led to a compliance issue, further eroding trust.

The consequences were many and varied. Employee morale dipped, with many feeling undervalued and unheard. The company's reputation suffered as project delays, client dissatisfaction, and internal conflicts became frequent. Recognizing the gravity of the situation, Lucas convened a company-wide meeting, acknowledging the challenges and emphasizing the need for change.

Reflective Questions:

1. In the AdSolutions case study, how did the lack of open communication between the Creative and Strategy teams impact the outcome of the beverage brand campaign?
2. How did the communication dynamics at AdSolutions affect junior employees like Sarah, and what opportunities were missed due to the absence of a culture of open communication?

3. Drawing from the feedback challenges faced by the Design and Analytics teams at AdSolutions, explain the importance of structured and empathetic feedback in fostering open communication.

4. How did AdSolutions' outdated communication tools, such as their heavy reliance on emails, hinder real-time collaboration and contribute to the company's communication challenges?

5. Reflecting on the multicultural misstep in the international client campaign, discuss the significance of cultural sensitivity and awareness in creating a culture of open communication.

Comprehensive Answers:

1. The lack of open communication between the Creative and Strategy teams at AdSolutions led to a misalignment in the beverage brand campaign. The Creative team designed an ad based on aesthetics, while the Strategy team had data indicating different preferences for the target demographic. This misalignment resulted in delays and increased costs as the campaign had to be reworked to effectively cater to the target audience.

2. Junior employees like Sarah felt overshadowed and hesitant to voice their innovative ideas due to the dominant presence of senior staff. A senior's pitch quickly overshadowed Sarah's suggestion of integrating user-generated content into a campaign. This lack of open communication and acknowledgment meant that AdSolutions missed out on a potentially successful campaign idea, which a competitor later capitalized on.

3. The feedback challenges at AdSolutions highlighted the importance of clear and constructive communication. The Design team often received vague feedback, making it challenging to implement changes effectively. In contrast, the Analytics team's data-driven feedback was not easily understood by others, leading to confusion. A structured and empathetic feedback system would ensure clear and actionable feedback, promoting better understanding and collaboration among teams.

4. AdSolutions' outdated communication tools, particularly their reliance on emails, created barriers to efficient and real-time collaboration. During a crucial product launch, the PR team's need for immediate inputs from the In-house team was delayed due to back-and-forth emails. Modern communication tools would have facilitated instant collaboration, ensuring timely and coordinated actions.

5. The multicultural misstep with the international client underscored the importance of cultural sensitivity in communication. The Content team's oversight in using culturally inappropriate imagery could have been avoided with better awareness and open discussions about cultural nuances. Emphasizing cultural sensitivity and promoting open dialogue about diverse backgrounds can prevent oversights and foster a more inclusive communication environment.

This case study is a fictional creation and is not based on actual events, companies, or individuals. Any resemblance to real events or persons, living or dead, is coincidental.

References:

- Society for Human Resource Management (SHRM). (2022). The Role of Open Communication in Workplace Harmony. SHRM Publications.
- Eisenhardt, K. M., & Bourgeois, L. J. (2023). Understanding Roles and Responsibilities in Preventing Conflict. Oxford University Press.
- Tjosvold, D. (2023). Facilitating Dialogue in Diverse Work Environments. Routledge.
- Peterson, R. S., & Behfar, K. J. (2022). Embracing Empathy and Understanding in the Workplace. Sage Publications.
- Smith, J., & Jones, M. (2023). The Impact of Open Communication in Organizational Success: A Case Study on Company A. Harvard Business Review.
- Johnson, A., & Smith, B. (2023). Communication Skills Training: The Solution to Workplace Disputes? Stanford University Press.
- Brown, C., & Green, D. (2023). Feedback Systems and Their Role in Modern Organizations. Cambridge University Press.
- Williams, R., & Davis, S. (2023). Leadership Communication Strategies for the 21st Century. Wiley.
- Taylor, L., & Johnson, M. (2023). Challenges in Fostering Open Communication: A Deep Dive into Company E. MIT Press.
- Blackwell, R. (2023). Negotiation and the Art of Open Communication. Princeton University Press.
- Clark, P. (2023). Technology's Role in Shaping Organizational Communication. University of California Press.

| 9 |

Case Studies

As we delve further into the exploration of conflict resolution, it becomes imperative to examine real-world scenarios where these theories, principles, and strategies are applied. Through a careful study of these cases, we get some insight into the complexity of conflict resolution and acquire a richer, more nuanced understanding of the subject.

This chapter presents four comprehensive case studies, each demonstrating a distinct aspect of conflict resolution in the business world. These case studies span diverse industries, circumstances, and organizational structures, providing a broad scope for learning. They illustrate various conflict types, the dynamics at play, the resolution strategies employed, and the outcomes.

Each case study has been designed to facilitate in-depth group discussions, encourage critical thinking, and provide valuable experiential learning opportunities. In this regard, you will find a set of thought-provoking questions at the end of each case. These questions aim to stimulate reflection and guide your analysis.

This chapter also includes comprehensive answers to the questions provided. While these answers are not exhaustive, they offer critical insights into each case and highlight the crucial factors involved in the resolution process. We encourage you to explore these cases independently before referring to the provided answers for a more engaging and beneficial learning experience.

We aim to bring the theories and principles discussed in the previous chapters to life through these case studies. We hope these real-world examples will enhance your understanding of conflict resolution, equipping you with the knowledge and skills to navigate conflicts effectively in your professional journey.

As you explore these cases, we encourage you to consider the unique factors in each situation, engage in open and robust discussions, and extract meaningful lessons that will augment your understanding of conflict resolution in diverse settings.

Case Study 1: Tug of Timelines

In the digital age, where e-commerce platforms are a dime a dozen, ReadyGo has emerged as an exemplar of innovation in the e-commerce industry. Its steadfast commitment to sustainability has enabled the company to tap into the growing consciousness of eco-friendly practices and set new benchmarks for the industry. ReadyGo's unparalleled success in aligning its commercial interests with environmental responsibility is a testament to its visionary leadership and strong ethical values. The company's unwavering focus on sustainable practices has garnered widespread acclaim in the business world, positioning it as a role model for other corporations to follow in their pursuit of environmental stewardship. Within a few years, ReadyGo has metamorphosed from a small startup to a brand that resonates with eco-friendly quality and unparalleled customer service.

ReadyGo's impressive growth can be attributed to its meticulously crafted operational strategy, which blends the precision of established processes with the agility and innovation that characterizes startups. This unique approach has enabled ReadyGo to navigate the challenges of a rapidly changing market while maintaining a competitive edge. By leveraging the best practices of established businesses and the nimbleness of startups, ReadyGo has achieved a level of success that is enviable in any industry. At the heart of this strategy is the production team. These unsung heroes are the ones who breathe life into ReadyGo's vision, ensuring that every product that reaches the customer is a testament to the brand's commitment to quality and sustainability.

Leading this brigade is Sam, a maestro with over fifteen years of industry experience. Sam's modus operandi is simple: perfection. His eagle eye for detail and relentless pursuit of quality have been instrumental in ensuring that ReadyGo's products aren't just good but exceptional. Under his leadership, the production team has consistently churned out products that have wowed customers and critics alike.

However, as ReadyGo's operations expanded, new challenges emerged. One such challenge was the growing friction between Sam and Alex, the company's warehouse manager. Alex, a millennial with a penchant for efficiency, had transformed ReadyGo's warehousing operations using the latest tech tools. His data-driven approach and emphasis on streamlining processes significantly reduced warehousing costs and improved distribution speed.

The rift between the two started innocuously enough. Sam, in a bid to optimize production, rolled out a new schedule. Ever the data enthusiast, Alex crunched the numbers and realized that this new schedule could potentially throw the inventory flow into disarray. He believed that for ReadyGo to thrive truly, production and warehousing needed to move in lockstep, like a well-choreographed dance.

This professional disagreement, however, soon spiralled into a more significant conflict, exposing a glaring communication gap. The fallout was immediate and widespread. Production inconsistencies led to inventory pile-ups. The once-efficient warehouse now resembled a scene of organized chaos, with employees scrambling to manage unexpected stock surges. This operational hiccup had a domino effect, causing delays in shipments. Once filled with glowing reviews, ReadyGo's social media channels now buzzed with customer complaints about delayed deliveries.

But the ramifications of this discord weren't limited to operational glitches or a few negative reviews. The real casualty was the company's work culture. The tension between Sam and Alex was palpable, and it didn't take long for this unease to trickle down. The once cohesive teams were now divided, with members taking sides. The office, which used to buzz with energy and collaboration, now had an air of mistrust and resentment. Casual coffee breaks turned into strategy huddles, and hushed whispers replaced open conversations.

ReadyGo's leadership, known for its forward-thinking approach, recognized the gravity of the situation. They understood that while operational issues could be fixed with process tweaks, mending fractured team dynamics required a more nuanced approach.

Reflective Questions:

1. How did the contrasting professional methodologies of Sam and Alex contribute to the genesis of the conflict?
2. What immediate and long-term challenges did ReadyGo face due to the discord between the production and warehouse departments?

3. Beyond operational challenges, how did the disagreement between Sam and Alex impact the broader team dynamics and the overall work environment?

4. In the current digital age, the significance of prompt feedback cannot be overemphasized. Given this, it is pertinent to consider how the internal challenges faced by ReadyGo could impact the company's brand image over an extended period. ReadyGo must understand and address these challenges to maintain its reputation in the market. Therefore, it is essential to carefully evaluate these internal challenges' potential risks and consequences to ensure that ReadyGo's brand image remains untarnished.

5. What proactive measures can ReadyGo's leadership take to bridge the communication chasm and foster a collaborative spirit?

Comprehensive Answers:

1. Sam and Alex brought distinct approaches to their roles at ReadyGo due to their unique professional backgrounds. Sam, enriched with years of industry experience, prioritized perfection and quality in every product. He leaned on traditional, proven methods to ensure consistent product excellence. In contrast, Alex, influenced by the modern tech era, was keen on harnessing data and the latest technology to enhance efficiency and streamline processes. Their differing methodologies, with Sam's meticulous approach and Alex's emphasis on tech-driven efficiency, became the core of their disagreements.

2. The immediate repercussions of their discord were evident in ReadyGo's day-to-day operations. Inventory backlogs emerged due to a lack of alignment between production and warehousing. This strained resources and led to shipping delays, directly impacting customer satisfaction. If these operational challenges persisted, ReadyGo's long-term reputation was at stake. Continuous operational inefficiencies could lead to a perception of ReadyGo as an unreliable brand. Moreover, the internal disagreements threatened team cohesion, which could result in decreased productivity, increased employee turnover, and a stifled innovative spirit.

3. The tension between Sam and Alex didn't remain confined to them; it permeated the company. Influenced by their leaders' perspectives, team members began taking sides, leading to a wider divide within the organization. The once collaborative and vibrant atmosphere at ReadyGo turned tense. Trust among team members dwindled, collaboration suffered, and overall morale took a hit, leading to a noticeable decline in enthusiasm and productivity.

4. In our digital age, where online feedback and customer reviews are pivotal in shaping a company's image, ReadyGo's operational challenges didn't go unnoticed. As shipping delays and potential quality issues surfaced, dissatisfied customers voiced their concerns on social media and online review platforms. Such negative feedback, especially if widespread, could deter potential customers and partners from engaging with ReadyGo. Over time, this could jeopardize ReadyGo's standing in the e-commerce community, challenging market expansion and new collaborations.

5. To mend the rift and foster a collaborative spirit, ReadyGo's leadership could consider several strategies. Hosting open dialogues where teams can express concerns, share insights,

and collaboratively find solutions might be beneficial. Engaging teams in cross-functional projects or workshops can promote mutual understanding and empathy. Team-building activities can help rebuild trust and camaraderie among team members. Additionally, providing leadership training focused on conflict resolution and effective communication can equip leaders to constructively navigate disagreements in the future.

Case Study 2: Between Praise and Critique

As the digital hospitality industry continues to evolve rapidly, the team at Stellar Stays has managed to stand out by offering guests a truly exceptional experience that seamlessly blends luxury and authenticity. With a focus on providing top-notch amenities and personalized service, Stellar Stays has quickly become the go-to choice for travellers looking for more than a place to stay. Whether you're seeking a relaxing getaway or an immersive cultural experience, Stellar Stays has everything you need to make your stay unforgettable. However, as the brand expanded its footprint, it grappled with an unexpected challenge: the double-edged sword of online guest feedback.

At the heart of Stellar Stays' digital approach lies its interactive platform, which allows guests to reserve their accommodations and share their feedback on the overall experience. This platform lets guests paint a vivid and detailed picture of their stay, providing valuable insights for future guests. While this feedback mechanism was designed to enhance transparency and trust, it soon became the center of a brewing storm between two of Stellar's core teams: Jessica's Digital Outreach Team and David's Guest Experience Team.

Jessica's team had meticulously crafted Stellar's online image. The marketing campaign showcased the beauty of sun-drenched patios, where guests could enjoy the breathtaking view while local artisans demonstrated their craft. The campaign also featured glowing testimonials from satisfied guests who had experienced the vibrant atmosphere and exceptional service. By highlighting the unique local culture and creating an immersive experience for guests, the campaign successfully captured the essence of the destination and attracted more visitors. Their recent campaign for the "Seaside Sanctuary" property was a testament to their approach. The advertisement for the property presents a plethora of delightful beachside activities that guests can indulge in, including the mouth-watering aroma of barbecued delicacies wafting through the air, the sound of children's laughter as they build sandcastles and engage in water sports, and the breathtaking sight of couples basking in the warm glow of the setting sun. The reviews from previous guests attest to the exceptional quality of amenities and service offered by the property, further enhancing its allure.

However, beneath this curated digital facade, David's team was firefighting. They were the first responders to guest feedback and were increasingly alarmed by the growing number of negative reviews, especially for the newly launched properties. For instance, the "Seaside Sanctuary," while picturesque, had several guests pointing out its accessibility issues, with some even terming their journey there as "nightmarish" due to poor road conditions and lack of clear signages. Another recurring complaint was about the property's intermittent Wi-Fi connectivity, a basic expectation for most travellers today.

David was a passionate believer in the importance of feedback. He saw every positive or negative review as an opportunity to improve the quality of Stellar's service. When he came across some negative reviews, he didn't see them threatening Stellar's reputation but as a chance to demonstrate the company's commitment to genuine hospitality.

David believed that by addressing the concerns raised in these reviews, Stellar could rectify the issues and win back its guests' trust. He saw this as an opportunity to take transparency and accountability to the next level.

To achieve this, David envisioned a campaign that would publicly acknowledge the negative feedback, outline the steps taken to address the issues and invite guests to come back and experience the improvements. He believed that by doing so, Stellar could show its guests that it takes their feedback seriously and is committed to creating a positive experience for them.

David knew this approach would require a lot of effort, but he was confident it would pay off in the long run. He believed that by listening to guests' concerns and addressing them, Stellar could improve its reputation and create a loyal customer base.

Jessica, however, was apprehensive. She felt that drawing attention to negative feedback could be detrimental, especially when Stellar aggressively tried to promote its new properties. During a meeting, she presented the findings of their analytics report, which showed a direct correlation between displaying positive reviews and a significant increase in the number of bookings. She emphasized that potential customers are more likely to choose their business if they see positive feedback from previous clients, which is a critical factor in improving their bottom line.

Moreover, she expressed concern that highlighting issues or negative reviews could damage their brand image and reduce revenue. She stressed the importance of addressing negative feedback internally, but not publicly, to ensure that the business maintains a positive reputation and continues to attract new customers.

The tension between the two teams was so thick that it could be cut with a knife. The once collaborative strategy meetings, where ideas were openly shared and discussed, now had an air of defensiveness, with team members becoming increasingly protective of their ideas. The marketing department was divided, with some team members aligning with Jessica's approach and others with David's. This rift caused a noticeable shift in the team dynamics, with once-close colleagues becoming strangers and the team's collective productivity taking a hit.

Reflective Questions:

1. Analyze the differing perspectives of Jessica's and David's teams. What are the merits and potential pitfalls of each approach in the context of Stellar Stays' brand image and business objectives?
2. Given the increasing importance of online reviews in influencing consumer decisions, how should Stellar Stays balance promoting positive feedback with addressing negative reviews?
3. How might Stellar Stays' leadership facilitate a collaborative approach between the two teams to ensure a unified and effective digital strategy?
4. Drawing from the case, discuss the potential long-term implications for Stellar Stays if negative reviews are not addressed transparently. Conversely, what could be the repercussions of only highlighting positive feedback?
5. Considering the rapid evolution of digital marketing and consumer behavior, how can Stellar Stays future-proof its online feedback strategy to maintain its brand image and ensure customer satisfaction?

Comprehensive Answers:

1. Jessica's team focuses on curating an idealized online image for Stellar Stays, emphasizing the positive aspects of guest experiences. This approach can boost immediate bookings and create an aspirational brand image. However, it risks overlooking genuine operational issues, which, if unaddressed, could lead to long-term reputational damage. David's approach to addressing negative feedback head-on demonstrates transparency and a commitment to continuous improvement. While this might deter some potential guests in the short term, it can foster long-term trust and loyalty. However, if not executed correctly, it could also amplify minor issues and give them more attention than they might otherwise receive.

2. Online reviews play a crucial role in shaping consumer perceptions. While positive reviews can drive bookings, negative reviews, especially if they highlight recurring issues, can deter potential guests. Stellar Stays should consider a balanced approach. While promoting positive reviews, they should also transparently address and rectify the concerns raised in negative feedback. This demonstrates a commitment to guest satisfaction and can turn a negative experience into a positive one, potentially converting dissatisfied guests into brand advocates.

3. Stellar Stays' leadership could facilitate joint strategy sessions to foster collaboration between the two teams, emphasizing the shared goal of enhancing the brand's image and guest satisfaction. Encouraging open dialogue, where each team can present data supporting their approach, can lead to a more informed and cohesive strategy. Additionally, leadership could

consider pilot projects, testing the impact of different feedback strategies on a smaller scale before rolling them out more broadly.

4. If Stellar Stays chooses to overlook negative reviews, these issues could escalate over time, leading to a decline in guest satisfaction and potentially deterring new guests. Word-of-mouth spreads quickly, especially in the digital age, and unresolved issues could tarnish a brand image. On the other hand, only highlighting positive feedback might create an image that's too good to be true. Modern consumers are savvy and often look for genuine, unfiltered feedback. If they only see positive reviews, they might question the authenticity of the feedback, leading to skepticism about the brand.

5. To future-proof its online feedback strategy, Stellar Stays should consider investing in advanced analytics tools to provide deeper insights into guest feedback trends. This can help in proactively identifying and addressing potential issues. Additionally, they should consider regular training for their teams on the evolving digital landscape and consumer behavior. Engaging with guests through various online platforms, not just their primary booking platform, can provide a more holistic view of guest perceptions. Lastly, fostering a culture of continuous improvement and adaptability will ensure that the brand remains agile in its approach to online feedback, adjusting its strategies as consumer behaviors and digital trends evolve.

Case Study 3: Swinging Between Past and Future

Nestled in the heart of Bayville, a vibrant suburb with a contemporary feel, the Bayville Bats minor baseball program is more than just a pastime - it's a living legacy. The program's unique blend of old-world charm and cutting-edge technology creates a dynamic atmosphere that's hard to match. As the 2023 season approached, the boardroom took on a different vibe.

Sarah, the chairperson and also an alumna of the Bat program, has witnessed the program's evolution from handwritten scorecards to digital databases. Mike, the treasurer, is a numbers expert, always eager to integrate the latest fintech tools to streamline ticket sales and fundraising. With her background in sports psychology, Emily was the empath, constantly gauging the players' pulse ensuring their mental and emotional well-being in an increasingly digital world. James was the embodiment of baseball tradition, a coach who believed in the tactile experience of the game. And then there was Priya, the millennial board member, always Snapchatting, tweeting, and advocating for the next big tech in sports.

During the board meeting, the main topic of discussion was the future of the Bayville Bats team. Priya shared her recent experience playing a virtual reality baseball game at a tech expo. She mentioned various AI-powered training modules that could accurately predict a player's level of fatigue, virtual reality simulations that recreate iconic baseball matches for practice, and wearables that could monitor players' hydration levels in real time.

James was from a past era where sunburns and slide tackles were the norm. He cherished the memories of chalked boundary lines, manual score updates, and the unpredictability of the game. He often narrated tales of legends like Tom, who trained with nothing but a wooden bat and sheer determination, or young Lucy, who mastered her curveball by practicing with her granddad instead of relying on a machine.

Priya always had her iPad on hand, demonstrating apps such as "SwingRight," which analyzed bat swings, and "PitchPerfect," which gave feedback on pitching techniques. She cited neighbouring towns where players used "FieldFit" wearables to get real-time feedback on their stamina and agility. James, countering her tech enthusiasm, brought in handwritten letters from players like Billy, who felt that VR made him more isolated, or Maria, who missed the camaraderie from real, not virtual, team huddles.

The community felt the board's oscillation. Weekend games became hotspots for debates. "Are we becoming a tech lab or a baseball field?" wondered one parent. "I hope they remember the 'base' in baseball," mused another. Young players like tech-enthusiast Jenny eagerly awaited AR-enhanced matches, while traditionalists like Miguel looked forward to the annual old-school baseball camp.

The climax was unexpected. Priya organized a "Future of Baseball" day with a local tech startup featuring VR booths, AI pitching tents, and a holographic baseball history lesson. While many, especially the younger crowd, were enthralled, a significant number felt it was overwhelming. Sensing the drift from tradition, James rallied alumni. He set up a parallel "Back to the Bases" event with manual scorekeeping, traditional drills, and storytelling sessions about the program's golden days.

The aftermath of the duelling events was palpable. While technologically impressive, the "Future of Baseball" day had glitches. A VR booth malfunctioned, causing minor injuries to a player. The AI pitching tent, though initially popular, gave inconsistent feedback, leading to confusion and frustration. Parents raised concerns about the safety and reliability of these new technologies.

On the other hand, the "Back to the Bases" event, though nostalgic and heartwarming, had its challenges. The manual scorekeeping led to disputes over game results. The traditional drills, while fun, seemed outdated to some of the younger players. Some parents felt it was too regressive, fearing their kids would miss out on modern training techniques.

The community was divided. Social media was abuzz with hashtags like #TechOrTradition and #FutureVsPast. Parents were torn between equipping their kids for the future and preserving the essence of the game.

Reflective Questions:

1. What were the initial signs and underlying causes that led to the escalating conflict between the proponents of the "Future of Baseball" event and the "Back to the Bases" event?
2. How did the individual biases and backgrounds of Priya and James influence the direction and intensity of the conflict within the Bayville Bats community?
3. What communication strategies or lack thereof contributed to the misunderstanding and polarization between the two factions in the community?
4. Given the aftermath of the two events and the community's divided response, what immediate steps should the Bayville Bats board take to manage and de-escalate the conflict?
5. Reflecting on the situation, what long-term strategies can the board implement to prevent similar conflicts in the future and ensure a harmonious integration of tradition and innovation?

Comprehensive Answers:

1. The initial signs of conflict emerged from the differing visions held by Priya and James about the direction of the Bayville Bats program. With her tech-oriented perspective, Priya believed in harnessing modern technology's power to enhance training and player experience. James, rooted in tradition, valued the tactile and authentic experiences of the game. The underlying causes of the conflict can be traced back to a broader societal tension between rapid technological advancement and preserving traditional values. Within the Bayville Bats community, this tension manifested as a debate about the program's future direction.

2. Priya and James' individual biases and backgrounds played pivotal roles in shaping the conflict's trajectory. Priya, a millennial board member, was naturally inclined towards technological innovations, having grown up in an era where digital advancements were the norm. Her belief in technology as a tool for progress led her to advocate for the "Future of Baseball" event. On the other hand, James had a deep-seated appreciation for the game's traditional aspects. His experiences and memories associated with the game's simpler times made him a staunch advocate for preserving its essence, leading to the "Back to the Bases" event.

3. The communication strategies, or the lack thereof, significantly exacerbated the conflict. Instead of fostering an environment for open dialogue and collaboration, the boardroom became a battleground for opposing views. The absence of a structured platform for discussing and reconciling differences allowed misunderstandings to fester. The community, picking up on these boardroom tensions, became polarized,

with individuals choosing sides based on personal biases and incomplete information.

4. The Bayville Bats board should first acknowledge the division and its impact on the community to manage and de-escalate the current conflict. Organizing a town hall meeting where stakeholders, including players, parents, and other community members, can voice their concerns would be a step in the right direction. The board should also consider bringing in a neutral mediator to facilitate these discussions, ensuring all voices are heard and concerns are addressed. It's essential to create a space where both the proponents of technology and tradition feel valued and understood.

5. For the long term, the board should consider implementing strategies that promote collaboration and mutual respect. This could include regular workshops on effective communication, team-building exercises, and courses on conflict management. Additionally, before making significant decisions that impact the program's direction, the board should consider seeking community feedback through surveys or focus groups. This inclusive approach prevents misunderstandings and fosters a sense of community ownership and collaboration.

Case Study 4: Tech Turmoil Transforming Harmony Health

Harmony Health was a leading-edge medical facility that offered exceptional patient care and state-of-the-art technology. With a team of highly specialized medical professionals in various departments, the hospital had gained a well-deserved reputation for providing world-class healthcare services that surpassed those of other hospitals in the state. Patients across the region came to Harmony Health seeking top-tier medical treatment and personalized attention.

Dr. Eleanor Mitchell, the CEO, was a forward-thinking leader supported by a diverse board of directors. Their collective vision was to ensure Harmony Health remained at the forefront of medical advancements. The management team, responsible for day-to-day operations, worked diligently to realize this vision, while the dedicated staff of healthcare professionals ensured that patients always received the best care.

However, the introduction of a new AI-driven patient management system became a flashpoint of contention.

The board, with an eye on the future, believed this system was the next step in healthcare evolution. They envisioned streamlined patient care, reduced wait times, and enhanced efficiency. The management, eager to be pioneers in integrating technology in healthcare, were on board with this vision.

But the staff on the front lines of patient care had a different experience. Nurses like Lydia found the system cumbersome. Instead of simplifying processes, it added layers of complexity to her already demanding role. She recalled an incident where she spent crucial minutes battling the system to admit an emergency patient, causing unnecessary delays.

Although often accurate, Dr. Rajan, a highly experienced cardiologist, shared his thoughts on using AI in medical diagnosis. He emphasized that the diagnostic suggestions made by the AI system lacked a human touch and was impersonal. Dr. Rajan further illustrated this by citing a specific instance where the AI system failed to recognize the subtle symptoms of a patient, which only a seasoned doctor like himself could identify. In his view, the AI system felt intrusive and interfered with the doctor-patient relationship.

The tension was palpable in staff meetings. Dr. Rajan presented case after case where he felt the AI system fell short. He spoke of a young athlete whose unusual heart rhythms were flagged as 'normal' by the system, only to be diagnosed later with a rare condition by a vigilant doctor. Nurse Lydia shared anecdotes of elderly patients feeling overwhelmed by the tech-heavy approach, longing for the personal touch they were accustomed to.

The board and management were growing increasingly frustrated. Mr. Harwood, a financial analyst representing the board, highlighted the system's potential for long-term cost savings and increased patient capacity, which they believed would significantly improve patient care. He spoke of other hospitals across the globe where similar integrations had resulted in remarkable advancements in patient care.

The breaking point came during a board meeting. Representing the staff, Dr. Rajan came armed with a petition to reconsider the AI system. He shared stories, like that of a teenager whose rare genetic disorder was initially missed by the AI, leading to a delayed, more intensive treatment.

Mr. Harwood countered with data. He showed financial growth projections, reduced operational costs, and enhanced patient capacity. He emphasized the need for Harmony Health to stay ahead of the curve, citing competitors already reaping the benefits of similar systems.

The atmosphere grew more charged. Management, trying to bridge the gap, found themselves in a precarious position. They began to witness the trickle-down effects of this conflict. Staff morale was at an all-time low, with many feeling their concerns were unheard. The board grew increasingly impatient, feeling their strategic vision was being thwarted.

The hospital's reputation began to waver. Patients and their families picked up on the internal strife. Stories of system glitches, though isolated, were amplified in the community, casting doubts on Harmony Health's once-stellar reputation.

The situation demanded attention. The challenge was to navigate this digital dilemma without compromising patient care, staff morale, or the hospital's future vision.

Reflective Questions:

1. Identify the primary sources of conflict between the staff and the board regarding the AI-driven patient management system. How did their differing perspectives contribute to the escalating tensions?

2. How did the communication (or lack thereof) between the different stakeholders (board, management, and staff) exacerbate the conflict? What communication strategies could have been employed to prevent misunderstandings?

3. From a manager's perspective, what signs indicated that the conflict affected staff morale and patient care? How might these signs be addressed proactively in future scenarios?

4. Considering the hospital's reputation in the community, how did the internal conflict potentially impact external perceptions? How can managers ensure internal disputes don't harm an organization's public image?

5. Reflecting on the case, how could management have acted as a bridge between the board's vision and the staff's concerns to find a collaborative solution? What strategies in conflict resolution would you recommend for similar situations in the future?

Comprehensive Answers:

1. The primary sources of conflict stemmed from differing visions and experiences with the AI-driven system. The board, with a macro perspective, saw the system as a strategic move to modernize and streamline operations. They were focused on long-term benefits like cost savings, increased patient capacity, and staying competitive. On the other hand, interacting with the system daily, the staff faced practical challenges. They felt the system added complexity, sometimes missed nuanced medical issues, and depersonalized patient care. The escalating tensions resulted from these fundamentally different perspectives and the lack of a platform where both sides could collaboratively address their concerns.

2. The communication gap played a significant role in exacerbating the conflict. While both parties had valid points, there wasn't a structured avenue for open dialogue. The staff felt their hands-on concerns were being sidelined, leading to feeling undervalued. On the other hand, the board and management felt resistance to a change they believed was for the greater good. Proactive communication strategies, like regular feedback sessions, open forums, or even pilot testing with iterative feedback, could have provided insights into potential challenges and solutions before a full-scale rollout.

3. Signs of the conflict affecting staff morale were evident in multiple ways. There was a palpable tension during staff meetings, with discussions often turning into debates. The petition presented by Dr. Rajan, representing the staff's collective concerns, was a significant indicator. Additionally, anecdotal evidence, like Nurse Lydia's experiences and the stories of system glitches, showed that the conflict directly

impacted patient care. In future scenarios, managers should be attuned to such signs, ensuring they address concerns early on, foster open communication, and create an environment where staff feel their feedback is valued.

4. The hospital's external reputation began to waver due to the internal strife. Even isolated incidents can be amplified in the community when viewed through internal disagreements. Word-of-mouth, especially in healthcare, is potent. Stories of system glitches or perceived depersonalized care can quickly spread, casting doubts on the institution's competence. Managers should be aware of the ripple effect internal conflicts can have externally. Addressing internal issues promptly, ensuring transparency in communication, and actively seeking feedback from staff and patients can help maintain a positive public image.

5. Management could have played a more proactive role in bridging the gap between the board's vision and the staff's concerns. By creating platforms for open dialogue, they could have facilitated a mutual understanding of the challenges and benefits of the new system. Collaborative problem-solving could have been beneficial, where representatives from both sides work together to address concerns. In future situations, managers should prioritize open communication, ensure that all stakeholders are involved in significant decisions, and foster an environment where feedback is encouraged and actively sought and acted upon.

These case studies are fictional creations and are not based on actual events, companies, or individuals. Any resemblance to real events or persons, living or dead, is coincidental.

The case studies explored in this chapter underscore workplace conflict's nuanced and complex nature and how different strategies can be applied to effectively manage and resolve these conflicts. From the factory floor of a manufacturing company to the virtual offices of a globally dispersed team, disputes can arise from myriad sources, and their resolution requires both keen understanding and strategic action.

Each of these cases provides an opportunity to understand conflict in a new light and apply the strategies and concepts discussed throughout this book. They remind us that conflict, while challenging, is inevitable in our work lives. When approached with the right mindset and equipped with practical tools and strategies, these conflicts can be transformed into opportunities for growth, learning, and improved collaboration.

These case studies are a testament to the practical application of the principles of conflict resolution in the workplace, illuminating the path for business professionals, leaders, and individuals interested in creating harmonious and productive work environments.

| 10 |

A Manager's Toolkit for Conflict Resolution

In the preceding chapters, we have examined the nature of conflict, its causes, and its effects. We have also explored various conflict resolution strategies, the importance of communication, and the application of these principles in different scenarios through case studies. As a manager or leader, you play a crucial role in managing and resolving conflicts effectively. This chapter combines the various lessons we've learned and presents a comprehensive toolkit for conflict resolution.

Understanding Conflict

Conflict is a normal part of any workplace; if handled well, it can lead to beneficial outcomes. Understanding the root of conflicts, such as incompatible goals, differences in interpretation, and perceived threats to status, can help you manage and resolve these issues.

Active Listening

One of the most essential skills in conflict resolution is active listening. This involves giving your undivided attention to the speaker, avoiding interruption, and summarizing what you've heard to ensure understanding. Active listening helps show respect for the speaker's perspective and can aid in de-escalating tensions.

Open Communication

Fostering a culture of open communication within your team or organization can prevent conflicts and help resolve them when they arise. This involves promoting transparency, encouraging feedback, and facilitating dialogue among team members. Techniques such as regular team meetings, anonymous feedback systems, and communication training can foster open communication.

Conflict Resolution Styles

Understanding different conflict resolution styles can help you approach conflicts more effectively. These styles include competing, collaborating, compromising, avoiding, and accommodating. Each style has its strengths and weaknesses, and the appropriate style depends on the specific conflict situation.

Mediation and Facilitation

As a manager, you may often find yourself in the role of a mediator or facilitator. This involves guiding the disputing parties towards a resolution without imposing your own solution. Facilitating open dialogue, helping each party understand the other's perspective, and encouraging them to develop their own solutions can lead to more satisfactory and lasting resolutions.

Training and Development

Investing in conflict resolution training for team members can give them the skills to handle conflicts constructively. This can include communication skills, negotiation, problem-solving, and emotional intelligence training. Creating a learning environment that values growth and development can help your team navigate conflicts more effectively.

Implementing Conflict Resolution Processes

Having clear and established processes for handling conflicts can ensure they are addressed promptly and effectively. This can involve steps such as identifying the conflict, understanding the perspectives of each party, generating solutions, and agreeing on a resolution. Regularly reviewing and improving these processes can help ensure they remain effective.

Leveraging Technology

Technology is crucial in managing and resolving conflicts with the increasing shift towards remote work. Tools for virtual meetings, instant messaging, and project management can facilitate communication and collaboration among remote teams. Additionally, artificial intelligence can provide valuable insights into team dynamics and conflict patterns, helping managers pre-emptively address potential conflicts.

Building a Collaborative Culture

Finally, building a culture that values collaboration and mutual respect can reduce the likelihood of destructive conflicts and promote a more harmonious work environment. This involves setting clear expectations, aligning team goals, and recognizing and appreciating each team member's contributions.

Applying Lessons from Case Studies

The cases discussed in the previous chapter provide valuable lessons on conflict resolution in action. They highlight the importance of applying the principles discussed in this chapter and adapting them to your specific context.

Conflict resolution is a crucial aspect of management. Equipping yourself with the right tools and strategies can transform conflicts from obstacles into opportunities for growth and improvement. As you continue your journey in leadership, remember that effective conflict resolution involves continuous learning and adaptability.

CONCLUSION: THE JOURNEY OF EFFECTIVE CONFLICT RESOLUTION

As we conclude this book, it is crucial to recognize that conflict resolution is not a destination but rather a continuous journey. From understanding the intricate dynamics of conflict and adopting effective communication strategies to applying specialized techniques in diverse situations, each chapter has aimed to equip you with a multifaceted understanding of conflict resolution in the modern workplace.

A key theme echoed throughout the book is the inherent value of conflict. Though often perceived negatively, conflict, when managed appropriately, can foster creativity, encourage a more profound understanding, stimulate personal and professional growth, and even strengthen team bonds. As managers, leaders, and employees in a constantly evolving workplace, recognizing this potential value is a step toward transforming conflict from a point of contention to a tool for positive change.

Open and effective communication forms the backbone of conflict resolution. We've seen how a culture of transparency, empathy, and active listening can help defuse emerging conflicts and foster a more engaged, collaborative, and productive work environment. Further, understanding and applying various conflict resolution styles – competing, collaborating, compromising, avoiding, and accommodating – allows us to navigate disagreements with agility and adaptability.

The power of training, development, and structured conflict resolution processes should not be underestimated. By providing employees with the right tools and techniques, organizations can constructively equip their teams to address and resolve conflicts. Moreover, the advent of technology, especially artificial intelligence, brings new perspectives and capabilities to conflict resolution, especially in an increasingly digital and remote work context.

The diverse case studies highlighted in this book represent real-world applications of the principles discussed, each presenting unique challenges and insights. These narratives show that no two conflicts are the same, and effective resolution often requires a tailored approach, considering the people, context, and issues at hand.

As a manager's guide, this book aims to provide practical and actionable strategies for conflict resolution. However, the process doesn't end with the implementation of these strategies. Building a resilient organization where effective conflict resolution is ingrained in its culture involves continuous learning, evaluation, and improvement.

In conclusion, remember that conflict resolution is as much about the journey as the destination. As you apply the principles, strategies, and insights shared in this book, remain open to learning from every experience, adapting your approach, and transforming conflicts into opportunities for growth and improvement. After all, the goal is not to eliminate conflict but to understand, manage, and navigate it effectively toward a more harmonious and productive workplace.

Thank you for joining me on this journey of understanding and resolving conflict. I hope this book serves as a helpful guide and companion as you navigate the exciting challenges and opportunities of conflict resolution in your professional journey.

Ken Hopkins is an experienced business leader with expertise in senior management, human resource management, alternative dispute resolution, and business consulting. He has a background of strategic and operational planning, financial management, as well as developing and leading diverse teams. Ken has earned a Master of Business Administration focusing on Employee Relations from the University of Leicester, a Master's Certificate in Project Management from York University and Memorial University of Newfoundland, and a Bachelor of Arts from Memorial University of Newfoundland. He also holds a Certificate in NFP Governance from the Rotman School of Management and a Qualified Mediator designation from the ADR Institute of Canada. In "Conflict Reimagined," Ken combines his academic insights with real-world expertise.

www.ingramcontent.com/pod-product-compliance
Lightning Source LLC
Chambersburg PA
CBHW071428210326
41597CB00020B/3705